Asset Allocation

Theory, Recent Developments and Beyond

nova science publishers
www.novapublishers.com

Business, Technology and Finance Series

Deepfake Technology Dilemmas: Mastering Managerial Navigation
Sanjay Taneja, PhD, Mukul Bhatnagar, Swati Gupta, PhD, Pawan Kumar, PhD, Sanjeet Kumar, PhD and Ercan Ozen, PhD (Editors)
ISBN: 979-8-89530-549-2
eBook ISBN: 979-8-89530-564-5

E-Finance: Transformative Strategies for Sustainable Development in the Digital Era
Sanjay Taneja, PhD, Ercan Ozen, PhD, Pawan Kumar, PhD and Reepu, PhD (Editors)
ISBN: 979-8-89530-230-9
eBook ISBN: 979-8-89530-376-4

Inclusive Business Approaches in Tourism: Stakeholder Engagement
Maximiliano E. Korstanje, Bindi Varghese, PhD, Joseph Chacko Chennattuserry, PhD, and Elangovan N., PhD (Editors)
ISBN: 979-8-89113-988-6
eBook ISBN: 979-8-89530-032-9

Digital Entrepreneurship: Future Directions
Rashmi Aggarwal, Tanvi Verma, Gurmeet Singh, PhD and Amandeep Singh, PhD (Editors)
eBook ISBN: 979-8-89113-737-0

Global Financial Analytics and Business Forecasting
Sanjay Taneja, PhD, Ercan Ozen, PhD, Pawan Kumar, PhD and Sanjeet Kumar, PhD (Editors)
ISBN: 979-8-89113-223-8
eBook ISBN: 979-8-89113-278-8

Green Management – A New Paradigm in the World of Business
Sanjay Taneja, PhD, Swati Gupta, PhD, Amandeep Singh, PhD, Mukul Bhatnagar and Arti Gaur (Editors)
ISBN: 979-8-89113-343-3
eBook ISBN: 979-8-89113-411-9

More information about this series can be found at
https://novapublishers.com/product-category/series/business-technology-and-finance/

Cemile Özgür
Vedat Sarikovanlik
Editors

Asset Allocation

Theory, Recent Developments and Beyond

nova
science publishers

www.novapublishers.com

DOI: https://doi.org/10.52305/DDBT4542

Library of Congress Cataloging-in-Publication Data

ISBN: 979-8-89530-649-9 (Softcover)
ISBN: 979-8-89530-721-2 (eBook)

Published by Nova Science Publishers, Inc. † New York

Contents

Preface

In the half century since the publication of Harry Markowitz's article on portfolio selection, modern portfolio theory (MPT) has been widely used for the management of investment portfolios. During this time, a basic understanding of the concepts and the mathematics of MPT has become established in the investment community. Despite the established knowledge of MPT, the fundamentals and practical applications of MPT are not widely recognized among users such as pension fund managers, institutional investors, or investment advisors. In 1952 Harry Markowitz pioneered the application of statistical methods to investment decision-making. Markowitz characterized risk as the variance of the distribution of probable future returns of an investment and showed how it is possible to choose a portfolio of different stocks that minimizes risk for a given level of expected return. Markowitz also showed how it is possible to calculate the efficient frontier, which represents the set of optimal portfolios that offer the highest expected return for a given level of risk or the lowest risk for a given level of return. These points are still the essence of MPT today although some refinements have been added recently.

As an investment tool, MPT informs decisions such as how to construct an optimally balanced investment portfolio. Similarly, the concept of efficient asset allocation as codified in MPT is considered the gold standard for investing, as its goal is to achieve the highest return for a given level of risk or conversely, the lowest risk, for a given return. MPT provides unprecedented insight into the trade-off between investment risk and reward, offering valuable guidance not only to retail shareholders but also professional investment advisors, who manage portfolios for a variety of clients ranging from individual private investors to large institutional investors such as pension funds, insurance companies, public funds like endowments, and corporations. MPT and portfolio selection models have been foundational in guiding both private and public sector investment portfolio strategies. Risk management strategies for extreme losses, particularly in the financial sector, have focused on quantifying the potential downside of a portfolio by the use of Value at Risk. Similarly, the concept of stress testing a portfolio against a variety of economic scenarios is widespread following the outbreak of the recent financial crises. In the decades since its discovery, MPT has been immensely influential in a broad array of academic disciplines and has become a centerpiece of modern finance. Given their adoption into industry best practices, insights on isolating systemic risk factors paid substantial dividends and account for the vast majority of revenue bases. However, most of the work involves the construction of static portfolios. In the years following, academics and practitioners alike began to question the validity of the static universe assumption and explored dynamic portfolio construction techniques. Though the exact details of these methods have changed substantially, much of the intuition has remained consistent over the years.

The analysis of risk within portfolio allocation is a fundamental subject of any finance textbook and specialist literature in portfolio management, investments, financial mathematics, and economics. The historical evolution of the main financial and mathematical principles has extremely deepened in the past years. Following alternative approaches, risk measurement has aroused growing interest in industry, companies, investment funds, banks, consulting firms, and academic world as well as new institutes devoted to research, so providing sound theoretical and practical methods to both measure and manage risk. While the assessment represented by value at risk (VaR) has significantly propelled in MPT over the past few decades, conditional value at risk (CVaR) as the effective dimensionality of the investment universe has increased and correlation structures have become more intricate. The theoretical properties of mean-variance and VaR portfolio optimization are well known and can be efficiently solved using quadratic programming. However, in practice, the distribution of the risk factor may not be normal and estimation errors proliferate as the sample size becomes limited.

The *homo economicus* idea and its critique according to neoclassical economic theory, the starting point in the analysis of economic phenomena is the actions of impersonal economic agents called "rational." In turn, rational behavior of economic agents is defined as follows: Actors are able to make a consistent choice, this ability is the primary characteristic of rational agents; moreover, it is assumed that they can consistently make decisions, which allow them to rank all possible actions and/or their consequences from best to worst; the ranking is based solely on their private experience and their level of well-being; the desires are derivative (that is, agents derive well-being from the fulfilment of desires), consistent (from any set of actions, several most favored ones can be consistently chosen), and they follow transitivity (well-being from fulfilled desire x is greater than or equal to that of unfulfilled desire y), and so on. It is also assumed that economic agents are perfectly experimental (the agent has complete knowledge of the utilities and probabilities over the uncertainties in the environment in which it operates) and they maximize (the agent chooses the available action that they believe will yield the greatest well-being, given their knowledge). Although it has long been thought that people are perfectly rational economic agents seeking the best possible utility, economic research has shown that human behavior deviates from this rationality. There are several behavioral gaps in decision-making that justify non-rational behavior. They showed that reasoning, in accordance with the assumptions of classical economics and the principle of rationality, is not so natural, and moreover, in many situations relatively rare.

In 1979, Daniel Kahneman and Amos Tversky unveiled prospect theory, revolutionizing the basis of decision-making under risk. This landmark theory outlines an empirical analysis of how choices are altered when outcomes are framed as gains or losses. These insights undermine the foundations of traditional expected utility theory by proposing that people value gains and losses asymmetrically, thereby altering preferences. Broadly speaking, economic agent models are theoretical frameworks used by economists to study how agents (e.g., consumers, firms, policymakers) make decisions under different conditions and constraints. A central tenet of economics asserts that individuals are utility-maximizing. Therefore, economic agent models attempt to explain how resources are allocated based on an individual's behavior and preferences. While this is a general notion that remains intact, what it means to be an economic agent has shifted over time. For much of economics' history, there was one prevailing model of how economic agents behave: Homo economicus. This framework posits that individuals are rational and seek to maximize their utility in order to optimize their outcomes. However, the wealth of empirical data that has been amassed since the mid-20th century has made it increasingly difficult to justify the homo economicus model. Thus, a growing number of economists have turned to "Behavioral Economics," an interpretative paradigm able to better explain the complex nature of human decision-making in economic contexts.

The first two chapters of this book present the main concepts and the theoretical backgrounds of portfolio asset allocation by delving deeper into MPT, alternative measures of portfolio risk and the incorporation of these measures into portfolio optimization framework. Chapter 3 focuses on behavioral portfolio management and discusses some of the main milestones in terms of the choice behavior of individuals under risk and uncertainty—namely, prospect theory, security–potential/aspiration theory, and behavioral portfolio theory. Additionally, the third chapter presents the methodology and empirical results of a unique experimental research in which portfolio asset allocations of individuals are obtained through laboratory experiments and predicted by a deep learning algorithm. Chapter 4 introduces the reader to the rank statistics and presents the results of a bibliometric analysis of the literature concerning the applications of ranks and/or rank statistics in the portfolio allocation context. The same chapter also reports empirical results of a research employing a recently proposed portfolio allocation strategy—namely, *rank based approach* (RBA)— that uses univariate as well as cross-sectional ranks of asset returns in portfolio allocation context. Furthermore, considering the recent developments in technology that have been transforming the finance industry and the asset allocation practices, Chapter 5 first introduces the reader to the fundamentals of machine learning and then offers a comprehensive literature review by evaluating over 150 published academic works that discuss the field of machine learning and/or apply algorithms in relation to various finance-related topics, such as the pricing of financial assets, algorithmic trading, managing financial risks, and portfolio asset allocation.

Overall, the content of this book covers both the traditional theory building up the foundations of asset allocation and the very recently proposed asset allocation strategies consisting of the applications of non-parametric rank-based approaches and machine learning algorithms. This will lead the reader from the theory and discussions of the past to today's innovative ideas, their applications, challenges, and prospects. We hope that the reader will enjoy the book!

Cemile Özgür, PhD
Vedat Sarikovanlik, PhD

March 15, 2025

Acknowledgments

We would like to thank the authors who have contributed to the book with their original and high-quality research. Moreover, we are grateful to Professor Belkıs SEVAL, who has many years of experience in academics as well as in finance industry, for reading the book and sharing her opinion about it. Finally, we also would like to thank the publishing team at Nova Science Publishers, without whom the book would not be able to reach the public.

Chapter 1

Modern Portfolio Theory

Merve Perçin*, PhD

Department of Finance, Istanbul University, Istanbul, Türkiye

Abstract

Harry Markowitz (1952, 1959) is regarded as the founder of modern portfolio theory, with his work in this field having revolutionized the world of finance. Markowitz argued that investment decisions should focus on more than the returns and risk levels of individual securities. According to him, the selection of assets in a portfolio should take into account the movements of each asset in relation to other assets—that is, their correlations. This suggests that an investment decision should be considered an optimization problem at the portfolio level rather than a matter solely concerning the performance of individual securities. Markowitz's work brought a more analytical and mathematical perspective to portfolio theory. He defined portfolio optimization as the trade-off between the average return and the variance (risk level) of a group of assets. According to this approach, investors should try to achieve two main objectives: maximizing the portfolio returns at a given level of risk and minimizing the portfolio risk at a given level of return. This two-way analysis provides a framework for investors to select the most appropriate portfolio based on their individual risk–return preferences. The most important innovation of this approach, which is known as the mean–variance model, is the focus on the performance of the portfolio as a whole, not on the individual assets. Markowitz argued that the selection of assets in a portfolio cannot be solely based on their individual characteristics. Instead, the relationship of each asset with the other assets (i.e., the correlation coefficient) should be considered a

* Corresponding Author's Email: merve.percin@istanbul.edu.tr

In: Asset Allocation: Theory, Recent Developments and Beyond
Editors: Cemile Özgür and Vedat Sarikovanlik
ISBN: 979-8-89530-649-9

fundamental element of investment decisions. This perspective contrasts with traditional approaches that focus solely on the analysis of individual assets and introduces a systematic approach to portfolio management. Markowitz's theory has rendered the process of making investment decisions more structured. Indeed, his approach provides a scientific framework to prevent investors from making irrational or emotional decisions. The mathematical optimization of portfolios allows investors to simultaneously control their risks and increase their returns. This theory also emphasizes the importance of diversification among financial assets (i.e., not putting all one's eggs in the same basket). As a result, Markowitz's work has laid an important foundation for modern financial theory and provided a systematic treatment of investment processes. Moreover, his mean–variance model has made a unique contribution to the investment world by showing that financial decisions should be governed not only by individual risks and returns but also by portfolio-level correlations.

Keywords: capital asset pricing model, risk and return, Markowitz portfolio diversification

1. Introduction

The central aim of economics is to manage the allocation of scarce resources in the most productive and optimal way. From both the microeconomic and macroeconomic viewpoints, a fundamental challenge for all economic participants—whether individuals, firms, or nations—is deciding how to distribute resources effectively. While this issue varies depending on the entity, it is commonly examined within the framework of portfolio theory. More specifically, modern portfolio theory provides a systematic approach that helps optimize allocation choices.

The origins of modern portfolio theory can be traced back to the influential studies by Harry Markowitz, which were published in 1952 and 1959. Widely recognized as the pioneer of this approach, Markowitz (1952) introduced a groundbreaking model that frames portfolio selection as a balance between the expected return and the expected risk, as measured by the variance. Known as the mean–variance model, this theory is built on two fundamental principles: achieving the highest possible return for a given risk level and minimizing the risk while maintaining a fixed return. These principles establish the "efficient frontier," a critical benchmark that assists investors in selecting portfolios that align with their individual risk–return preferences. An important contribution of Markowitz's work is that it shows that investors should not focus solely on the characteristics of individual securities. Instead, he emphasized that the interactions of each asset with other assets should also be considered. This approach brought a systematic perspective to portfolio management.

Many theories have been developed based on the mean–variance model. One is the financial asset pricing model (FVPM), which is widely used in the pricing of financial assets today. The FVPM was introduced independently by Sharpe (1964), Lintner (1965), and Mossin (1966), albeit during the same time period. In the following years, the model was further developed through the contributions of Black (1972), Treynor (1961, 1965), and other scientists. In this chapter, we will first focus on the basic elements, assumptions, derivations, and criticisms of the mean–variance model, which serves as the basic building block for modern portfolio theory. Then, in the second section, the FVPM, which was developed as an extension of the mean–variance model, will be discussed in detail.

2. The Utility Function and Indifference Curves

Utility theory, which was developed in the field of economics, provides a basic framework for modeling the risk and return concepts in finance. Here, utility refers to the level of satisfaction obtained by an individual as a result of consuming or possessing a good or service. In this context, the total level of satisfaction obtained by consuming all the units of a good is termed the "total utility" (TU), while the increase in satisfaction provided by each additional unit consumed is known as the "marginal utility" (MU).

The relationship between total utility and marginal utility can be analyzed alongside the quantity of consumption (Q). To help understand the behavior of the utility function, Figure 1 reveals how these two concepts interact. According to Figure 1, the total utility initially increases, although the rate of increase slows down over time. This process continues until point Q_0, after which the total utility starts to decrease. By contrast, when the marginal utility function is analyzed, it is seen that the marginal utility has a positive value until point Q_0 but then gradually decreases. After Q_0, the marginal utility shifts into the negative region and continues to decline. This means that if the consumption amount of an individual exceeds Q_0, the total utility will decrease.

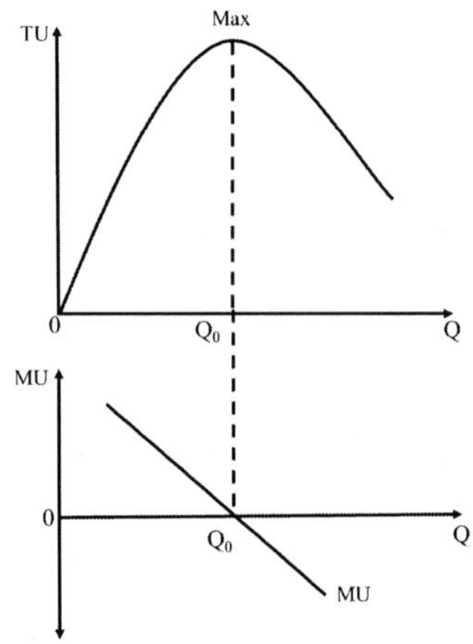

Source: Author's own illustration.

Figure 1. Total Utility (TU) and Marginal Utility (MU).

A rational individual should limit the amount of consumption at point Q_0 to maximize the level of satisfaction (utility). This point is the equilibrium level at which the individual maximizes the total utility. Otherwise, an increase in the amount of consumption will lead to a decrease in the individual's total utility. This relationship provides an important clue as to how consumption decisions should be optimized and serves as a critical reference point for both economics and finance applications.

Utility theory is typically analyzed under two main headings—namely, cardinal utility theory and ordinal utility theory. These two theories differ significantly from each other in terms of their assumptions and approaches. Cardinal utility theory assumes that utility can be quantified and expressed numerically. According to this theory, the utility derived from one product does not change due to the consumption of other products. Furthermore, utility is considered to be an objective concept; therefore, if different individuals consume the same amount of a good, the utility that these individuals obtain will be the same. Due to this understanding of objective measurement, cardinal utility theory makes it possible to analyze consumer behavior mathematically. However, this theory has encountered some difficulties and shortcomings in the real world due to its assumption regarding the measurability of utility.

Ordinal utility theory criticizes the assumptions of cardinal utility theory and argues that utility cannot be measured mathematically. According to ordinal utility theory, the utility an individual obtains from one good changes according to the consumption of other goods. For example, the utility derived from consuming bread alone may differ from that derived when jam is consumed alongside bread. Moreover, utility is a subjective concept and differs from person to person. Thus, the utility levels of individuals who consume the same good will differ from each other. Ordinal utility theory argues that individuals can rank goods according to their level of utility, although this utility cannot be expressed as a precise quantitative value.

The main difference between the two theories lies in their approach to whether utility is measurable. Cardinal utility theory allows for analyses of consumer equilibrium based on the assumption that utility is measurable. However, this assumption has created many problems in practice and caused the theory to have limited use. Conversely, ordinal utility theory provides a more flexible framework by assuming that utility is immeasurable and so has found a wider area of application in fields such as economics and finance.

In the field of finance, the influence of ordinal utility theory is quite evident. Based on this theory, it is accepted that the main objective of rational individuals is to maximize the utility obtained through consumption. In addition, it is stated that individuals also consider the risks they may face while making their decisions. According to this perspective, as individuals have different attitudes toward risk (i.e., risk averse, risk neutral, or risk loving), the utility function of each individual will also be different. In Figure 2, the utility functions of three individuals with different attitudes toward risk are visualized. This figure allow us to understand more clearly how individuals optimize their decisions in line with their risk perceptions. When Figure 2 is analyzed, it can be seen that individuals' attitudes toward risk can be classified under three main headings—namely, risk-averse individuals, risk-indifferent individuals, and risk-seeking individuals. The aggregate utility curves of these three groups differ according to their responses to an increase or decrease in their wealth.

Risk-seeking individuals are risk takers who focus on the possibility of gain. The aggregate utility curve of these individuals has a steeper structure when compared with other individuals. This means that the benefit they gain from a one-unit increase in their wealth is greater than the loss of utility caused by a one-unit decrease in their wealth. In other words, for these individuals, the satisfaction provided by the gain is more dominant than the discomfort caused by the loss. Thus, the main motivation of risk-seeking individuals is based on taking advantage of earning opportunities.

Risk-indifferent individuals are those who do not care about the risk factor or who have a neutral approach. For these individuals, the total utility gain from a one-unit increase in wealth is equal to the total utility loss from a one-unit decrease in wealth. Put simply, these individuals have a symmetric attitude toward gains and losses. The utility curve of risk-indifferent individuals has a flat slope due to this feature.

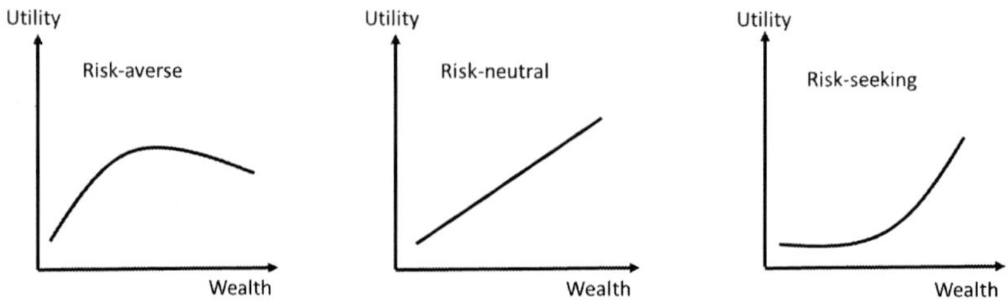

Source: Author's own illustration.

Figure 2. Total Utility Graphs of Individuals.

Risk-averse individuals constitute the most risk-sensitive group. For these individuals, the benefit brought about by a unit increase in their wealth is lower than the loss of benefit caused by a decrease of the same amount. Risk-averse individuals prioritize protecting themselves from losses over making gains. Therefore, the total utility curve of these individuals has a more horizontal structure. The main concern of risk-averse individuals is avoiding the negative effects of uncertainty. It is generally assumed that rational individuals tend to be risk-averse to some degree. This reflects their inclination to avoid potential losses during decision making. However, the degree of this tendency may vary from person to person. Risk perception and the related attitudes are considered an important factor shaping an individual's financial goals and strategies.

The following example illustrates the impacts of attitudes toward risk in a complex business investment scenario.

A group of entrepreneurs are offered two investment options with different risk and return profiles. The investments involve partnering in a technology start-up. The entrepreneurs must decide on an option based on their attitude toward risk. The investment options are as follows:

- *Low-risk investment*: The entrepreneur invests in a 10% stake in the company. The guaranteed annual return on this investment is a fixed amount of 50,000 TL. Even if the company's performance deteriorates, the entrepreneur's principal is safe, although the expected annual return will never exceed this amount.

- *High-risk investment*: The entrepreneur invests 10% in the company's project to develop a new product. With this option, the entrepreneur has:
  - 40% probability: The product is successful and the annual return reaches 200,000 TL.
  - 60% probability: The product fails and the entrepreneur does not realize any return; the entrepreneur may even lose the initial investment.

Expected Return = (0.40 x 200.000) + (0.60 x 0) = 80,000 TL (1)

Although the high-risk investment seems more attractive than the low-risk investment in terms of the expected return, individuals' attitudes toward risk affect their decisions:

- *Risk-indifferent individual*: This entrepreneur will remain indifferent concerning the two options. Although the expected return is not equal between the low-risk and high-risk investments, the possibility of loss or gain does not affect the entrepreneur's decision.
- *Risk-seeking individual*: This entrepreneur will choose the high-risk investment. This individual finds the possibility of a high return more attractive than a low return. Even the possibility of investment failure does not dissuade the entrepreneur from making this decision, because the prospect of a large gain provides more satisfaction.
- *Risk-averse individual*: This entrepreneur will prefer the low-risk investment. Despite the high return potential, the possibility of failure is an unacceptable risk for this individual. The assurance provided by the guaranteed 50,000 TL is most important to this entrepreneur.

This complex scenario shows that individuals make decisions by considering not only the expected return but also their tolerance for uncertainty and their perception of risk. In the business world in particular, attitudes toward risk stand out as a critical factor shaping entrepreneurs' investment strategies and long-term success.

The assumption that utility is a subjective concept underpins ordinal utility theory, which has led to the emergence of indifference curves. Indifference curves are an important analytical tool used in contemporary microeconomics to visualize consumer preferences and budgetary constraints.

These curves represent a consumer's choice of two combinations of goods that provide the same level of satisfaction and utility. The consumer is equally indifferent to all the combinations of goods on this curve (i.e., the consumer does not prefer any one combination over another).

A key property of indifference curves is that they are generally curved inward toward the origin. This reflects the idea that consumers face a decreasing marginal rate of substitution between goods, meaning that they are willing to sacrifice less of one good as they acquire more of another. Additionally, the assumption that indifference curves do not intersect is based on the premise that consumer preferences remain consistent. Another fundamental assumption is that indifference curves farther from the origin represent higher levels of satisfaction or utility on the part of the consumer.

Indifference curve analysis plays a central role in the assessment of marginal rates of substitution (MRSs) and opportunity costs. The MRS refers to the quantity of one good that a consumer is willing to sacrifice in exchange for an additional unit of another good. This ratio is used as a critical indicator when analyzing consumer behavior. Moreover, indifference curves are one of the building blocks of consumer equilibrium analysis. The intersection of a budget line and an indifference curve indicates the point at which a consumer reaches the maximum utility within their budget. This analysis is an important tool for both understanding individual consumer behavior and deriving market demand curves.

Although indifference curves are widely used in microeconomics, they have been subject to various criticisms. One of the most important such criticisms is that the theory often relies on unrealistic assumptions about human behavior. For example, the assumption that consumer preferences remain constant over time may not correspond to dynamic preferences in the real world. Hence, consumers' changing needs and wants over time may limit the practical use of indifference curves. Moreover, indifference curve analysis may be inadequate for multidimensional combinations of goods, given that it focuses on simple combinations of two goods. In real life, consumers are often interested in more than one good or service, which increases the complexity of the analysis.

While indifference curves are an effective tool for modeling and analyzing consumer behavior, they should be treated with caution due to their limitations and the criticisms leveled against them. When used with an awareness of the assumptions and limitations, indifference curves can provide a powerful framework for economic analysis. However, the development of more complex models that consider dynamic consumer behavior and real-world variables may require going beyond indifference curve analysis.

Consider a university student. This student has two different sources with which to prepare for an exam: a textbook and online video lectures. The student thinks that the information in the textbook and the information provided via the online video lectures are of equal benefit. As a result, the student is indifferent when it comes to choosing between studying for two hours by reading a textbook or watching an online video lecture for one hour. Both options enable the student to achieve the same level of success in preparing for the exam. In this case, for the student, the following combinations can be visualized on the same indifference curve:

- 4 hours textbook + 1 hour online video
- 2 hours textbook + 2 hours online video
- 1 hour textbook + 3 hours online video

The slope of the indifference curve represents the MRS, which indicates how much the student is willing to give up in terms of one study method to gain more of the other when deciding between the two study methods. Moving along the curve, one can observe how the student gives up video viewing time in order to have more textbook reading time (and vice versa). This example demonstrates how the student distributes their time, ensuring that the benefit gained from both methods is equal. This type of analysis represents an important tool for understanding consumer behavior in areas such as resource allocation and time management.

In Figure 3, the x-axis represents the video, while the y-axis represents the textbook. At points A and B, the individual shows indifference between the combinations of (video, textbook), meaning that points A and B both provide the same level of utility (U_3) to the individual. As their income increases, the individual typically adjusts their consumption because they can afford more goods, thereby moving to an indifference curve farther from the origin. This results in a higher level of utility. In Figure 3, the individual with a higher income reaches a higher utility level (U_2) at point C when compared with points A and B, as they can access more combinations of (videos, textbooks).

When we consider the utility function within the framework of financial investment decisions, it is possible to formulate the utility function as a function of the expected return and risk.

$$U = f(E(r), \sigma) \tag{2}$$

U: The benefit to be obtained by the investor
E(r): Expected return
σ: The risk of the occurrence of returns

As a result, the indifference curves will vary among individuals with different levels of risk aversion (see Figure 4). Still, it is important to remember that at every point on the same indifference curve, the total benefit derived by the individual remains constant.

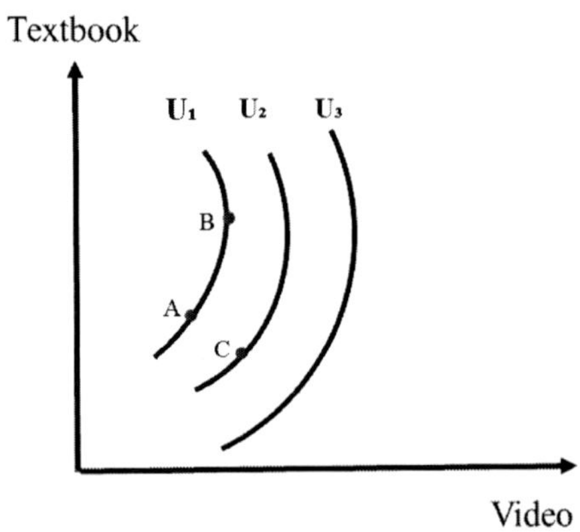

Source: Author's own illustration.

Figure 3. Indifference Curves of the Risk Averse Individual.

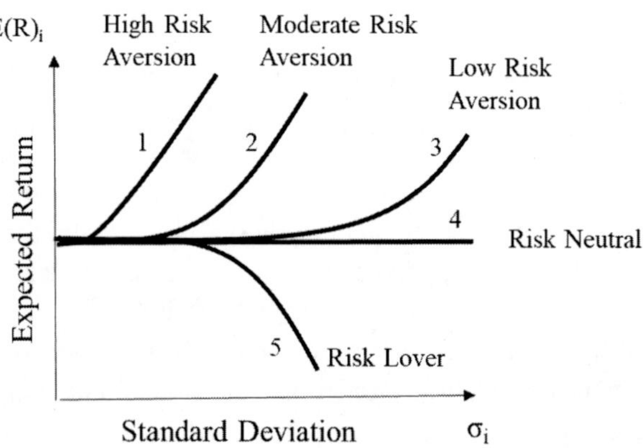

Source: Author's own illustration.

Figure 4. Indifference Curves of Individuals with Different Attitudes towards Risk.

3. The Mean–Variance Framework

Until the 1950s, the traditional portfolio approach was widely used in financial markets. Indeed, while this approach does not have a scientific basis, it was used extensively by investors. The primary goal was to create a portfolio with securities selected from different sectors and to maximize returns. However, in 1952, the publication of a paper titled "Portfolio Selection" by Harry Markowitz marked a turning point in the world of finance. This paper introduced the modern portfolio theory developed by Markowitz (1952), which earned him the Nobel Prize in Economic Sciences in 1990.

The key assumptions of modern portfolio theory are as follows:

1. *Rational investors*: All investors make investment decisions in a logical and analytical manner.
2. *Investment decisions based on the expected return and* risk: Investors make decisions solely based on the anticipated returns and the risks associated with those returns.
3. *Risk and return relationship*: Investors prefer higher returns for a higher risk, whereas for the same return, they prefer a lower risk.
4. *Return distribution*: Returns are assumed to follow a normal distribution.
5. *Efficient capital markets*: The markets are considered to be efficient, meaning that all the available information is instantly reflected in the asset prices.
6. *Measuring risk:* The past returns' standard deviation is the sole measure of risk.
7. *Market participants*: There are many market participants, none of whom have sufficient market share to influence the overall market movement.
8. *Low-cost information access*: Information about securities is available at a low cost.
9. *Institutional structure*: The institutional structure of the markets is highly developed and regulations ensure the stability of the markets.

One of Markowitz's major contributions was the integration of both returns and risks. Modern portfolio theory emphasizes that investors should consider not only the returns and risks of individual securities but also the relationships between securities and the tendency for securities to move together. The measure of these relationships is typically the correlation coefficient, which is a critical factor in minimizing portfolio risk.

The most important strategy for reducing portfolio risk is diversification. Accurately measuring the correlation among securities is essential for effectively implementing a diversification strategy. In this context, examining the relationships between the securities in a portfolio is vital for understanding and managing the associated risk.

Markowitz's theory has generated tangible and applied results, not just theoretical ones. The objective and mathematical methods introduced by modern portfolio theory have shaped investment decisions within a more scientific framework, which has laid the groundwork for subsequent portfolio theories and provided investors with a more systematic perspective. Therefore, modern portfolio theory has not only enabled investors to make more efficient and rational decisions but also caused a revolution in the fields of financial analysis and risk management.

4. The Efficient Frontier and Optimal Portfolios

Modern portfolio theory has introduced significant concepts to the financial literature, including the key concepts of the *efficient frontier* and *efficient portfolios*. In financial markets, an unlimited number of portfolios can be created using all the available financial assets, and this collection of portfolios forms the opportunity set for an investor. However, according to Markowitz (1952, 1959), the criterion for selecting the most optimal portfolio from this set is explained through the concept of "efficiency." In this context, efficiency refers to the idea that investors should select portfolios that either deliver the highest expected return for a specific level of risk or minimize the risk for a given level of expected return.

Efficient portfolios are those that maximize the expected returns for a given level of risk or minimize the risk for a specific return level. The choice between these portfolios depends on the investor's risk preferences; however, in all scenarios, efficient portfolios represent the best possible trade-off between risk and return. According to Markowitz's theory, investors should focus solely on selecting efficient portfolios, given that such portfolios provide either the highest return for a given amount of risk or the lowest risk for a specified return.

The curve formed by the combination of efficient portfolios is known as the efficient frontier. Hence, the efficient frontier shows the curve of portfolios that provide the best possible risk–return trade-offs. This curve helps investors identify the most optimal combinations of risk and return. For example, it shows the highest return achievable for a given level of risk or the lowest risk achievable for a given level of return. Every point on the efficient frontier represents a different risk–return balance. The main purpose of efficient portfolios and the efficient frontier itself is to present the most optimal portfolio combinations for investors, considering not just the returns of individual financial assets but also the interrelationships among those assets. In this context, efficient portfolios incorporate diversification strategies that reduce the risk and make the best use of the diversity within financial markets.

To better understand these concepts visually, graphs of efficient portfolios and the efficient frontier are often used. An efficient portfolio is represented by a point on the efficient frontier, with this point indicating the portfolio that provides the maximum return for a given level of risk. The efficient frontier is the curve that connects all the efficient portfolios, representing the best possible choices for managing risk and return (see Figures 5 and 6). Thus, efficient portfolios and the efficient frontier offer investors the ability to make the most optimal decisions for managing risk and return. Modern portfolio theory provides a mathematical and statistical framework for analyzing these concepts, allowing investors to make better investment decisions. The theory emphasizes that investors should not rely on selecting individual assets but instead engage in portfolio diversification to optimize their investment strategy, enhancing both their returns and their safety.

According to modern portfolio theory, the process for selecting the optimal portfolio applies the following logic. From the portfolios located on the efficient frontier, the investor will choose the one that maximizes their utility. In other words, the optimal portfolio for an investor is found where the tangent point between the efficient frontier and the investor's highest utility indifference curve intersects. Investors with different levels of risk aversion (and, consequently, different indifference curves) will choose distinct optimal portfolios from the efficient frontier. The efficient frontier represents the set of portfolios that provide the best possible return for a specific level of risk. However, each investor has a unique tolerance for risk (or level of risk aversion), meaning that they assess risk and return differently. This is reflected in the indifference curve, which shows the combinations of risk and return that leave an investor indifferent.

By contrast, an investor's indifference curve shows the trade-offs they are willing to make between risk and return. A steeper curve indicates a higher aversion to risk, while a flatter curve indicates less concern regarding risk. An investor will aim to select the portfolio that gives them the highest possible utility, which is represented by the tangent point between their indifference curve and the efficient frontier. The optimal portfolio for an investor is found at the point where the indifference curve is tangent to the efficient frontier. This point represents the portfolio with the best balance of risk and return for the investor's specific risk tolerance. As each investor has a different risk profile, each will choose a different point on the efficient frontier as their optimal portfolio.

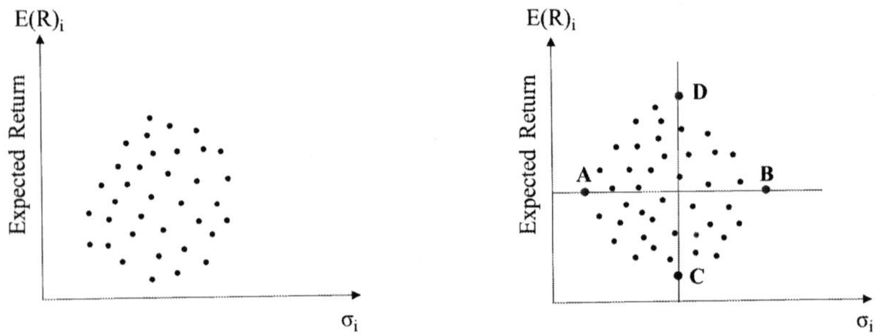

Source: Author's own illustration.

Figure 5. Opportunity Set and Selection of Efficient Portfolios.

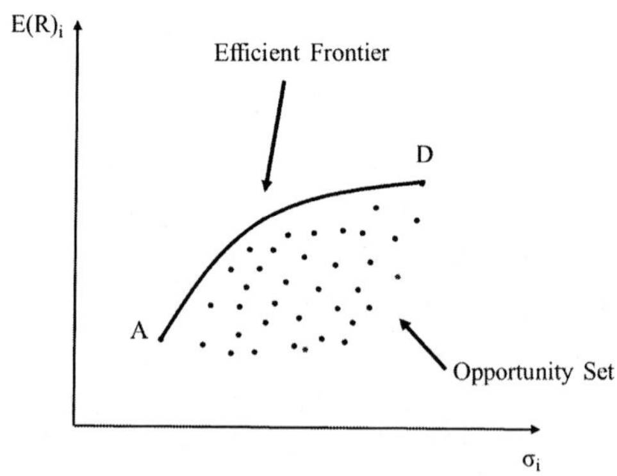

Source: Author's own illustration.

Figure 6. The Efficient Frontier.

Investors with different degrees of risk aversion will have different indifference curves, leading to different optimal portfolios:

- *Risk-averse investors*: Investors with higher risk aversion will have steeper indifference curves, meaning that they will choose a portfolio closer to the lower-risk, lower-return portion of the efficient frontier.
- *Risk-seeking investors*: Conversely, investors with lower risk aversion will have flatter indifference curves, leading them to select a portfolio higher up on the efficient frontier, with potentially higher returns but also a higher risk.

To sum up, the optimal portfolio is not a one-size-fits-all solution. It is individualized and depends on the investor's personal risk preferences and utility function, as determined by the point where the investor's indifference curve is tangent to the efficient frontier.

5. Tobin's Portfolio Model

James Tobin's work, published in 1958, provided a critical expansion of Markowitz's mean–variance model, challenging some of its core assumptions and introducing key modifications that enhanced the original theory. According to Markowitz's model, an investor's opportunity set, or the collection of assets available for investment, is made up exclusively of risky assets. However, Tobin disagreed with this. He argued that the investment universe is not limited to risky assets. Instead, he proposed that investors can also include assets with very low or zero risk, often referred to as risk-free assets, such as cash or government bonds.

In Tobin's model, investors are encouraged to diversify their portfolios by incorporating both risky and risk-free assets. This diversification helps reduce the overall risk by offering a hedge against uncertainty, providing investors with a way to optimize their portfolios based on their individual preferences and levels of risk tolerance. Tobin (1958) introduced a two-step decision-making process for portfolio construction, wherein each phase is independent:

1. *First step: Distribution between risky and risk-free assets:* In the first stage, the investor decides how to divide their portfolio between risky and risk-free assets. This choice is driven by the investor's risk preference—that is, how much risk they are willing to accept in pursuit of potentially higher returns. For example, those with a lower tolerance for risk would likely allocate a larger share to risk-free

assets, while investors who are more tolerant of risk may choose to put a higher percentage into risky assets.

2. *Second step: Selection of risky assets:* In the second stage, the investor focuses on the risky component of the portfolio. This step involves selecting the specific risky assets and determining the optimal mix of those assets. Markowitz's efficient frontier is used in this process. Tobin (1958) emphasized that the efficient frontier provides a range of portfolios that offer the best trade-offs between risk and return. The key insight derived from Tobin's framework is that the investor must identify the single portfolio on the efficient frontier that is optimal. This optimal portfolio is not subjective; rather, it is the same for every investor, regardless of their individual risk preferences.

The introduction of a risk-free asset into the portfolio construction process alters the portfolio optimization landscape. A risk-free asset, such as a Treasury bill, is an investment that carries no default risk and has a known return with zero volatility (i.e., its standard deviation is zero). The addition of such an asset reduces the overall risk of the portfolio without sacrificing the level of return, enabling investors to achieve a more favorable risk–return trade-off.

This modification leads to the development of the *capital market line* (CML), a straight line that connects the risk-free asset and the efficient frontier. The CML represents the set of optimal portfolios that combine both risky and risk-free assets. By shifting from a portfolio consisting solely of risky assets to one that includes a mix of both types of assets, investors can create portfolios that offer the best possible risk–return combinations based on their preferences. The CML provides a visual representation of the highest return achievable for a given level of portfolio risk, incorporating the risk-free asset into the analysis.

The CML starts at the risk-free asset (with zero risk and a fixed return) and extends upward through the efficient frontier. The point at which the CML tangentially touches the efficient frontier marks the optimal portfolio. This optimal portfolio is considered the best option for investors, given that it offers the maximum return for any given level of risk. By combining both risky and risk-free assets in the correct proportions, investors can choose a portfolio that aligns with their specific risk preferences. The introduction of the CML and the optimal portfolio has simplified the decision-making process for investors. Due to the ability to combine risk-free assets with risky assets, the investor has greater flexibility in achieving the desired risk–return profile. This model makes it easier for investors to identify the portfolio that will provide the best balance between risk and expected return, regardless of their individual risk tolerance.

Tobin's (1958) work significantly enriched modern portfolio theory by incorporating risk-free assets into the analysis of portfolio construction. Indeed, his approach altered the way investors view portfolio optimization, enabling them to include both risky and risk-free assets to create more diversified and optimized portfolios. The result was the creation of the CML, which has provided a clearer way for investors to identify the optimal portfolio based on their risk preferences.

Tobin's contribution was pivotal in rendering portfolio theory more accessible and practical for real-world applications. It has provided investors with a more comprehensive framework that not only addresses the need for diversification but also incorporates the possibility of risk-free assets into the investment process, thereby enhancing the overall effectiveness of portfolio management strategies. By improving the decision-making process, Tobin's model laid the groundwork for more robust and rational investment choices.

The risk of a portfolio consisting of both risky and risk-free assets is written as follows:

$$\sigma_P^2 = w_i^2\sigma_i^2 + (1 - w_i)^2\sigma_{rf}^2 + 2w_i(1 - w_1) \cdot \sigma_i\sigma_{rf}\rho_{i,rf} \quad (3)$$

As the standard deviation of the risk-free asset (σ_{rf}) is equal to zero, the standard deviation of the portfolio can be written as follows:

$$\sigma_P = w_i \cdot \sigma_i \quad (4)$$

σ_p: Standard deviation of portfolio
σ_i: Standard deviation of risky asset i
σ_{rf}: Standard deviation of risk-free asset
$\rho_{rf,i}$: Correlation coefficient between risky asset and risk-free asset
w_i: Weight of risky asset i in the portfolio
The expected return of the portfolio can be expressed as follows:

$$E(R_p) = w_i \cdot E(R_i) + (1 - w_i)R_f \quad (5)$$

$E(R_p)$: Expected return of portfolio
$E(R_i)$: Expected return of risky asset i

R_f: Return of risk-free asset

When we include the equality we found in Equation 4 in Equation 5, we reach the following equality:

$$E(R_P) = \frac{\sigma_P}{\sigma_i} E(R_i) + \left(1 - \frac{\sigma_P}{\sigma_i}\right) R_f \tag{6}$$

$$E(R_p) = R_f + \frac{[E(R_i) - Rf]}{\sigma_i} \sigma_P \tag{7}$$

In Equation 7, it is shown that a portfolio consisting of a risk-free asset and risky assets can be written as a linear equation. The point at which the line intersects the axis is R_fR_f, while the slope of the line is $\frac{E(R_i)-R_f}{\sigma_i}$. Utilizing this information, the asset combination line for risky asset A and the risk-free asset is drawn as follows:

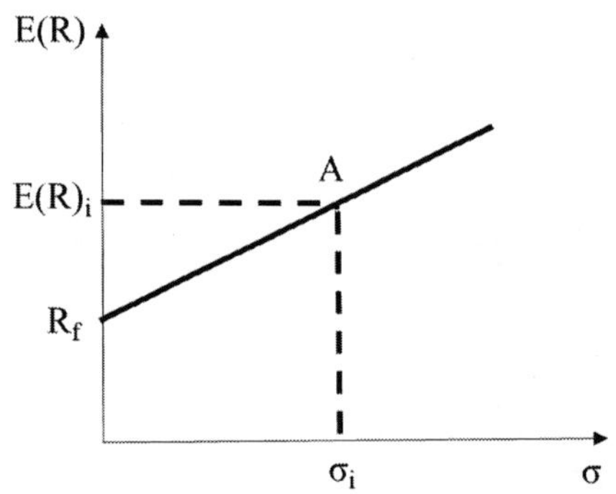

Source: Author's own illustration.

Figure 7. Portfolio Containing Risky Asset (A) and the Risk-Free Asset's Combination Line.

Below, in Figure 8, three different portfolios, labeled A, B, and C, are presented and the selection of the optimal portfolio is explained.

In Figure 8 presented above, the curve depicted with a thicker line illustrates the efficient frontier as defined in Markowitz's mean–variance model. This frontier represents the set of optimal portfolios that offer the highest expected return for a given level of risk, or equivalently, the lowest risk for a given level of expected return. When examining Figure 8, it becomes evident that among the portfolios labeled A, B, and C, only portfolio C is tangent to the efficient frontier. This tangency indicates that portfolio C is the most optimal choice from among the three, because it aligns with the principles of efficiency in terms of portfolio selection.

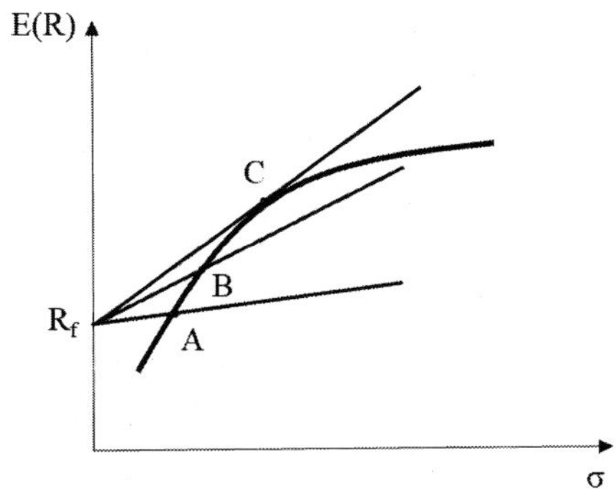

Source: Author's own illustration.

Figure 8. Combination of Risk-Free and Risky Assets.

Furthermore, when indifference curves—representing investors' preferences and risk tolerance—are added to the figure, they illustrate how individuals with varying risk appetites select their portfolios. More specifically, the points along the R_fC line where these selections occur are shown in Figure 9, providing insights into the decision-making process of investors with different attitudes toward risk. By analyzing the indifference curves of individual A, it becomes apparent that individual A exhibits a stronger aversion to risk than individual B. According to Markowitz's mean–variance model, in a scenario where the investment universe is limited to only risky assets, individuals A and B would allocate their investments at points A_1 and B_1, respectively, on the efficient frontier. These points represent the optimal portfolios for these individuals based on their respective levels of risk tolerance and expected returns.

However, when Tobin's (1958) portfolio selection theorem introduces a risk-free asset into the opportunity set, the investment decisions of both individuals undergo significant changes. More specifically, individual A adjusts their portfolio from point A1 to point A2, while individual B transitions from point B1 to point B2. This shift reflects an improvement in utility for both individuals, as they each move from a lower utility level (U_1) to a higher utility level (U_2).

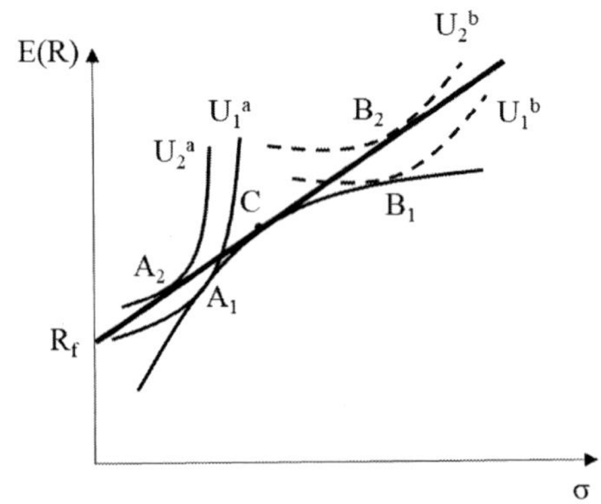

Source: Author's own illustration.

Figure 9. Optimal Portfolio Selection According to Tobin.

Due to individual A's more risk-averse nature, they allocate a greater proportion of their portfolio to the risk-free asset, effectively constructing a lending portfolio, which sits among the portfolios located between the risk-free rate (R_f) and point C on the capital allocation line (CAL). In contrast, individual B, who is less risk averse and exhibits a higher tolerance for risk, prefers a portfolio with leverage. By borrowing funds, individual B selects a portfolio beyond point C on the CAL, ultimately arriving at point B2. This difference in investment strategies highlights how varying attitudes toward risk influence portfolio composition and asset allocation.

The CAL represents the trade-off between a risky portfolio and a risk-free asset, with its slope determined by the Sharpe ratio of the selected portfolio. In contrast, the CML is a specific form of CAL that connects the market portfolio to the risk-free asset, where its slope corresponds to the Sharpe ratio[1] of the market portfolio. While the CAL accounts for the total risk, the CML focuses solely on the market portfolio assets and provides the most efficient risk–return balance. Every portfolio along the CML is deemed optimal, whereas the CAL can be drawn for any given risky portfolio. Ultimately, the CAL reflects individual investor choices, whereas the CML defines the most efficient investment approach in the market.

[1] The Sharpe ratio is a performance metric that measures the risk-adjusted return of an investment. Developed by William F. Sharpe, it is calculated by dividing an investment's excess return (i.e., the return above the risk-free interest rate) by its total risk (i.e., the standard deviation).

6. Capital Asset Pricing Model

The capital asset pricing model (CAPM) is a financial theory that defines the relationship between the systematic risk—also referred to as the market risk or non-diversifiable risk—and the expected return of an asset or investment. It offers a framework that links the required return on an investment to the associated level of risk in a linear manner. The CAPM plays a crucial role in finance because it helps measure the systematic risk of financial assets, and it is widely used for pricing risky securities. The model also aids in calculating the expected returns on assets while factoring in both their risk levels and the cost of capital.

The CAPM, despite facing some criticisms, has its foundations deeply rooted in Markowitz's modern portfolio theory. Markowitz's theory introduced the concepts of portfolio diversification and risk minimization, which laid the groundwork for future models in the finance field. Thus, one of the key models developed following Markowitz's theory is the CAPM, which was independently formulated by William F. Sharpe in 1964, John Lintner in 1965, and Jan Mossin in 1966. Over time, this model was further refined and expanded upon by various scholars, including Fischer Black and Jack Treynor, which contributed to the evolution of the CAPM.

In Markowitz's original model, there is an assumption that investors are risk averse, meaning that they are inclined to avoid risk when making investment decisions. Additionally, his model assumes that investors focus primarily on two parameters when choosing their portfolios—namely, the mean (expected return) and the variance (risk) of the returns. As a consequence, investors are anticipated to choose an "efficient portfolio" that either achieves the highest expected return for a certain level of risk or reduces the risk for a given level of expected return. This approach, which links the expected return and the risk in a statistical manner, is referred to as the "mean–variance model."

To further elaborate on the mean–variance model's efficient portfolio, Sharpe (1964) and Lintner (1965) introduced two key assumptions to Markowitz's model. The first assumption, referred to as the "homogeneity of expectations," posits that investors, under the same initial market conditions, concur regarding the joint distribution of asset returns over a given investment period. This assumption suggests that all investors share the same view of the market expectations, which forms the basis for testing the model. The second assumption introduces the notion of unlimited borrowing and lending at a risk-free rate, implying that all investors have the ability to borrow and lend any amount of capital at the same risk-free rate, which is assumed to be consistent throughout the market. These two assumptions laid the foundation for the CAPM and provided a structure for assessing how investors can balance risk and return in their portfolios, making the CAPM one of the most widely accepted models in modern financial theory.

7. Criticisms of Modern Portfolio Theory

Since the second half of the 20th century, modern portfolio theory (MPT) has made invaluable contributions to the understanding of financial markets and investment strategies. However, it has also faced a number of criticisms that question its applicability and assumptions in real-world scenarios. These criticisms highlight the limitations that may reduce MPT's practical use in some contexts.

One of the primary criticisms revolves around the assumption that the expected returns are normally distributed. In reality, asset returns do not perfectly follow a normal distribution, as financial markets often exhibit skewed distributions with heavy tails (i.e., extreme events occur more frequently than normal distributions would predict). This assumption fails to account for the possibility of extreme market movements or "black swan" events that are not captured by a normal distribution.

Another point of contention is the model's assumption that all investors operate under the same single-period investment horizon. In real life, the investment landscape is dynamic, and investors often make decisions based on multiple time periods, each with varying levels of risk and expected returns. Critics have argued that applying MPT to a multi-period investment context may lead to inaccurate or overly simplistic conclusions, given that it fails to address how changing market conditions over time may affect portfolio performance.

Additionally, the assumption that all individuals are rational actors—making decisions solely based on maximizing utility and minimizing risk—has been criticized for not accurately reflecting human behavior. In practice, investors often display cognitive biases, emotions, and irrational decision-making, which the model does not account for. Behavioral finance has provided insights into how real-world investors deviate from rationality, thereby challenging the assumptions underlying MPT. Furthermore, MPT's restrictive assumption that investors must invest solely in risky assets or risk-free assets has been questioned. In reality, investors often combine both types of assets based on their individual risk preferences, financial goals, and other factors. Thus, the model does not fully account for the flexibility and diversity of investment choices available in practice.

Finally, the practical application of MPT involves various forecasting and technical challenges. For example, accurately predicting the correlations between different assets, determining the optimal weights for diverse asset combinations, and accounting for changing market conditions are all complex tasks. The model's reliance on precise estimates for these variables can introduce significant errors, as real-world data are often imperfect and subject to change. Consequently, MPT may not always provide reliable predictions when applied to dynamic financial markets. These criticisms highlight the limitations of MPT when making practical investment decisions and highlight the necessity of more sophisticated models that can more accurately represent the complexities of both financial markets and human behavior.

References

Black, F. (1972). Capital Market Equilibrium with Restricted Borrowing. *Journal of Business*, *45*(3), 444–454.

Fama, E. F., & French, K. R. (2004). The Capital Asset Pricing Model: Theory and Evidence. *Journal of Economic Perspectives*, *18*(3), 25–46.

Lintner, J. (1965). The Valuation of Risk Assets and the Selection of Risky Investments in Stock Portfolios and Capital Budgets. *Review of Economics and Statistics*, *47*(1), 13–37.

Markowitz, H. (1952). Portfolio Selection. *Journal of Finance*, *7*, 77–91.

Markowitz, H. (1959). *Portfolio Selection: Efficient Diversification of Investments*. Wiley.

Mossin, J. (1966). Equilibrium in a Capital Asset Market. *Econometrica*, *35*, 768–83.

Sharpe, W. F. (1964). Capital Asset Prices: A Theory of Market Equilibrium under Conditions of Risk. *Journal of Finance*. *19*(3), 425–442.

Tobin, J. (1958). Liquidity Preference as Behavior Towards Risk. *Review of Economic Studies*, *25*(2), 65–86. https://EconPapers.repec.org/RePEc:oup:restud:v:25:y:1958:i:2:p:65-86.

Treynor, J. L. (1961). Market Value, Time, and Risk. *Unpublished manuscript*, Rough Draft dated 8/8/61, #95–209.

Treynor, J. L. (1965). How to Rate Management of Investment Funds. *Harvard Business Review*, *43*, 63–75.

Chapter 2

Measuring Risk: Alternative Definitions and Portfolio Allocation

Mahammad Charkasov*, PhD

Department of Economics and Management, Khazar University, Baku, Azerbaijan

Abstract

This chapter conducts a comprehensive examination of modern approaches to measuring and managing risk in terms of portfolio allocation. It begins by highlighting the limitations of variance-based risk models, particularly when it comes to capturing asymmetric return distributions and tail events. The discussion then introduces several downside risk measures, including the value at risk (VaR), conditional value at risk (CVaR), drawdown-based metrics, and lower partial moments, offering a detailed analysis of their theoretical foundations, computational complexities, and practical implications. Building on these measures, this chapter explores how they can be incorporated into portfolio optimization frameworks—ranging from minimum VaR and minimum CVaR strategies to drawdown-constrained allocations. Particular attention is paid to the ways in which these approaches address fat-tailed market risks and improve capital preservation during periods of high volatility or market stress. The empirical examples provided demonstrate the comparative behaviors of the different methodologies, shedding light on how each measure performs under various market conditions. Next, the final sections review current industry applications, discussing how institutions such as banks, hedge funds, insurance companies, and pension funds integrate downside-focused risk metrics into their investment decision-making processes. The real-world

* Corresponding Author's Email: mcharkasov@khazar.org

In: Asset Allocation: Theory, Recent Developments and Beyond
Editors: Cemile Özgür and Vedat Sarikovanlik
ISBN: 979-8-89530-649-9

challenges, including data scarcity, model validation, and computational demands, are also examined, along with emerging trends such as machine-learning-driven risk analytics and the incorporation of environmental, social, and governance (ESG)-related factors into traditional models. Overall, this chapter provides a practical and theoretical guide for investors, risk managers, and researchers seeking to adopt robust, tail-sensitive strategies in relation to modern portfolio management.

Keywords: downside risk measurement, portfolio optimization, tail risk, asset allocation, risk management

1. Introduction

The measurement and management of risk have become increasingly sophisticated in modern portfolio theory (MPT) and practice. As financial markets evolve and new challenges emerge, the need for robust and comprehensive risk assessment methodologies continues to grow. This chapter explores various approaches to risk measurement and their applications in portfolio allocation, providing both theoretical foundations and practical insights.

Risk measurement lies at the heart of asset allocation, influencing how investors and institutions build portfolios to balance expected returns against uncertainty in financial markets. Early MPT (Markowitz, 1952) popularized the use of variance (or the standard deviation) as a primary risk metric, under the assumptions of normally distributed returns and mean–variance optimization. However, real-world market conditions often deviate from these idealized assumptions, highlighting the need for alternative definitions of risk that better capture asymmetric losses, tail events, and drawdowns (Jorion, 2007; Artzner et al. 1999).

This chapter systematically examines three key aspects of risk measurement and portfolio allocation. First, it explores the downside risk measures, including the value at risk (VaR), conditional value at risk (CVaR), and drawdown analyses. These measures provide different perspectives on portfolio risk and have distinct mathematical properties that render them suitable for various investment contexts. Second, this chapter investigates optimal risk portfolios, focusing on how these risk measures can be incorporated into portfolio optimization frameworks. Finally, this chapter reviews the current applications, bridging the gap between theoretical developments and practical implementations.

The content of the present chapter is particularly relevant for investment professionals, risk managers, and researchers seeking to understand both the theoretical underpinnings and the practical applications of modern risk measurement techniques. It provides insights into how different risk measures can be effectively utilized in portfolio construction and management, considering the real-world constraints and implementation challenges.

The remainder of this chapter is organized as follows. Section 2 presents a comprehensive overview of the downside risk measures, examining their mathematical properties, advantages, and limitations. Section 3 then explores optimal portfolio construction using these risk measures, including the minimum VaR, minimum CVaR, and optimal drawdown portfolios. Sections 4 and 5 conclude the chapter with a review of the current applications, featuring case studies and practical implementations across different market environments and institutional settings.

2. Downside Risk Measures

The evolution of downside risk measures represents a paradigm shift in terms of how the investment community conceptualizes and measures risk. This development emerged from the growing recognition of the limitations of traditional variance-based approaches, particularly in the context of increasingly complex financial markets and sophisticated investment strategies.

The journey began with Markowitz's (1952) mean–variance framework, which revolutionized portfolio theory by providing a mathematical foundation for risk measurement. However, as the financial markets continued to evolve, practitioners and researchers increasingly questioned the framework's underlying assumptions. Roy (1952), contemporaneously with Markowitz, introduced the "safety-first" criterion, marking one of the earliest formal recognitions that investors might care differently about downside volatility and upside volatility.

The limitations of variance as a measure of risk became particularly evident during the market crises of the 1970s and 1980s. Traditional variance-based approaches assume symmetric return distributions and rational investor behavior regarding both gains and losses. However, empirical evidence has consistently demonstrated that financial returns exhibit fat tails and negative skewness (Mandelbrot, 1963; Fama, 1965). Moreover, behavioral finance research, notably the study by Kahneman and Tversky (1979), revealed that investors exhibit asymmetric preferences concerning gains and losses, with losses having a more significant psychological impact.

The 1990s marked a turning point, with the widespread adoption of the VaR by financial institutions, catalyzed by the introduction of JP Morgan's RiskMetrics methodology in 1994. The VaR seemed to offer a more intuitive way to quantify the downside risk, expressing potential losses in monetary terms rather than through abstract statistical measures. However, the limitations of VaR became apparent during the Asian financial crisis (1997) and the Russian default (1998), leading to the development of the CVaR by Artzner et al. (1999), which addressed some of the VaR's theoretical shortcomings.

The 2008 global financial crisis further exposed the inadequacies of traditional risk measures and accelerated the development of more sophisticated approaches. The crisis highlighted the importance of considering the tail risk, the correlation breakdown during stress periods, and the limitations of models based on normal distribution assumptions. These issues led to regulatory changes, notably Basel III, which emphasized the need for more comprehensive risk measurement approaches.

Recent developments in terms of computing power and data availability have enabled the implementation of more sophisticated downside risk measures. For instance, machine learning techniques and big data analytics are now being integrated into risk measurement frameworks, allowing for the more nuanced capture of market dynamics and tail events (Cont, 2010).

2.1. Methodological Deep Dive

The implementation of downside risk measures requires careful consideration of the available methodological approaches, each of which is associated with distinct advantages and challenges. This section examines the primary methodological frameworks used when calculating downside risk measures, with particular attention paid to their practical implications and data requirements.

2.1.1. Parametric Approaches

Parametric methods rely on assumptions regarding the underlying return distributions, typically assuming normal or Student's t-distributions. For the

VaR calculation, the parametric approaches use the mean (μ) and standard deviation (σ) of the returns, along with a confidence level multiplier (α). This method's primary advantage lies in its computational efficiency and straightforward implementation. However, as demonstrated by Duffie and Pan (1997), parametric approaches may underestimate the risk during periods of market stress when the returns deviate significantly from the normal distribution assumptions.

2.1.2. Non-Parametric Approaches

Historical simulation represents the most widely used non-parametric approach. This methodology makes no assumptions regarding the underlying distribution, instead relying on actual historical data to estimate the risk measures. McNeil and Frey (2000) demonstrated that historical simulation captures fat tails and other market characteristics more effectively than parametric methods. However, this approach faces challenges related to the limited availability of historical data, especially for new financial instruments or during regime changes.

2.1.3. Monte Carlo Simulation

Monte Carlo methods offer a flexible framework for risk measurement by generating numerous scenarios based on historical data or theoretical assumptions. As highlighted by Glasserman (2003), such methods are particularly valuable when dealing with complex portfolios or non-linear instruments such as options. This approach allows for the incorporation of various market factors and correlation structures, although the computational intensity remains a significant consideration.

2.1.4. Data Requirements and Practical Considerations

2.1.4.1. Sample Size and Frequency

The choice of sample size and data frequency significantly impacts the accuracy of risk measures. Danielsson and De Vries (2000) suggested that high-frequency data may improve tail risk estimation, although practitioners must balance this against the increased noise and computational demands. The typical requirements include the following:

- Daily VaR: 250–500 days of historical data
- Monthly VaR: 3–5 years of monthly returns

- Stress testing: Data covering multiple market cycles

2.1.4.2. Tail Data Availability

Extreme value theory (EVT) provides a framework for dealing with limited tail data. McNeil et al. (2015) demonstrated how EVT can improve tail risk estimation, particularly for high confidence levels (e.g., 99% VaR), where historical data may be sparse.

2.1.4.3. Implementation Challenges

Several practical challenges have emerged when implementing these methodologies:

1. *Time-varying volatility*: Generalized autoregressive conditional heteroskedasticity (GARCH) models and other volatility-updating schemes help address the non-constant nature of market volatility, although they introduce additional model risk and complexity.
2. *Correlation dynamics*: Traditional correlation estimates may break down during periods of stress. However, dynamic conditional correlation (DCC) models, as proposed by Engle (2002), offer one approach to address this challenge.
3. *Model validation:* Regular backtesting becomes crucial for validating risk measurement approaches. The Basel Committee framework provides standards for VaR model validation, although similarly rigorous frameworks for other risk measures are still evolving.

2.2. Comparative Analysis of Downside Risk Measures

In MPT and risk management, various downside risk measures have emerged, each with distinct characteristics and applications. Hence, this section provides a comprehensive comparison of the primary downside risk measures, examining their mathematical foundations, practical implications, and implementation considerations. Table 1 provides a useful tool for the comparative analysis of downside risk measures.

Table 1. Comparison of Downside Risk Measures

Measure	Calculation Method	Advantages	Disadvantages	Typical Applications
Value at Risk (VaR)	Historical simulation, parametric (variance-covariance), or Monte Carlo simulation.	– Simple to communicate and widely used. – Benchmark for regulatory purposes.	– Does not capture the magnitude of losses beyond the cutoff. – Highly sensitive to model assumptions.	– Regulatory capital requirements. – Basic downside risk monitoring and reporting.
Conditional VaR (CVaR)	Usually estimated via simulations or optimization-based approaches.	– Addresses VaR's shortcomings by focusing on the tail beyond VaR. – More coherent measure (subadditive).	– Computationally more complex. – Still depends on the confidence level choice and data quality.	– Risk management in portfolios with heavy tails. – Setting tail-risk constraints in asset allocation.
Maximum Drawdown	Observed historically using time series of portfolio values.	– Easy to interpret in a historical context. – Highlights large sustained losses.	– Backward-looking; does not predict future drawdowns. – Ignores frequency or duration of drawdowns.	– Performance assessment for hedge funds, mutual funds. – Stress testing under extreme market conditions.
Lower Partial Moments (e.g., LPM1, LPM2)	Integration of the loss function (below a target) over the probability distribution.	– Captures the shape of downside distribution more comprehensively. – Flexible in defining thresholds.	– Harder to communicate to non-technical audiences. – Can be more complex to estimate in practice.	– Custom risk metrics for specific return floors. – Supplementary analysis where normality assumptions fail.

This table provides a comprehensive comparison of the key characteristics, advantages, disadvantages, and application requirements of various downside risk measures. Information on the mathematical underpinnings, practical implications, and computational complexity of each risk measure are included in the table. This information will help investment managers and risk specialists determine the most appropriate risk measurement approaches for their portfolio management.

2.2.1. Value at Risk

The VaR represents the maximum potential loss at a given confidence level over a specified time horizon. As defined by Jorion (2007), the VaR is expressed mathematically as follows:

$$VaR_\alpha = \inf\{\, l \in R : P(L > l) \leq 1 - \alpha\} \qquad (1)$$

where L represents the loss distribution, α is the confidence level, and VaR_α provides a threshold beyond which losses are considered extreme.

Using the parametric (variance–covariance) approach, the VaR can be estimated as:

$$VaR_\alpha = \mu - Z_\alpha \cdot \sigma \qquad (2)$$

where μ represents the expected return of the portfolio, σ is standard deviation of the returns, and Z_α is the critical value derived from the standard normal distribution (e.g., $Z_{0.95}$ =1.645 for a 95% confidence level).

The VaR has become a standard risk measure in the financial industry, particularly following its inclusion in the Basel regulatory framework. Moreover, Duffie and Pan (1997) demonstrated its effectiveness in providing a single, comprehensive measure of the market risk. The implementation of the VaR offers several advantages, including intuitive interpretation and widespread regulatory acceptance. However, as Artzner et al. (1999) noted, the VaR fails to satisfy the mathematical property of subadditivity, making it potentially problematic for portfolio optimization.

Advantages:

- Intuitive interpretation for non-technical stakeholders
- Widely accepted by regulators and institutions
- Simple to communicate and implement

Drawbacks:

- Not a coherent risk measure
- Fails to capture the tail risk beyond the threshold
- May underestimate the risk during market stress

Computational complexity:

- Low to moderate for parametric approaches
- Moderate for historical simulation
- High for Monte Carlo methods

2.2.2. Conditional Value at Risk

The CVaR, also known as the expected shortfall (ES), measures the expected loss beyond the VaR threshold, making it a more informative measure of the tail risk. Following the approach of Acerbi and Tasche (2002), the CVaR is defined as follows:

$$CVaR_\alpha = E[L|L \geq VaR_\alpha] \tag{3}$$

This captures the average loss in the tail of the distribution, addressing one of the VaR's key limitations.

For a normal distribution, the CVaR is computed as follows:

$$CVaR_\alpha = \mu - \frac{\phi(Z_\alpha)}{1-\alpha} \tag{4}$$

where $\phi(Z_\alpha)$ is the probability density function of the standard normal distribution.

The CVaR provides a more conservative risk assessment by considering the average loss beyond the VaR threshold. McNeil et al. (2015) demonstrated that the CVaR is particularly effective in capturing the tail risk during periods of market stress.

Advantages:

- Coherent risk measure
- Captures the tail risk effectively
- More stable than the VaR for optimization

Drawbacks:

- More complex to explain to stakeholders
- Requires more data for accurate estimation
- Sensitive to outliers in historical data

Computational complexity:

- Moderate for parametric approaches
- Moderate to high for historical simulation
- Very high for Monte Carlo methods

2.2.3. Maximum Drawdown

The maximum drawdown (MDD) measures the largest peak-to-trough decline in the portfolio value over a specific period. Mathematically, as presented by Grossman and Zhou (1993), it is expressed as follows:

$$D(t) = \max_{s \in [0,t]} V(s) - V(t) \tag{5}$$

$$MDD = \max_{t \in [0,T]} D(t) \tag{6}$$

where $D(t)$ is the drawdown value at time t and $V(t)$ is the portfolio value at time t.

The MDD is particularly relevant for investors concerned about capital preservation, as it reflects the largest observed loss in value. Unlike the VaR and CVaR, the MDD is a time-dependent metric, meaning that it is influenced by historical market conditions.

Advantages:

- Path-dependent measure
- Captures sequential losses
- Particularly relevant for fund managers

Drawbacks:

- Highly sensitive to the sample period

- May not be representative of the future risk
- Difficult to use for optimization

Computational complexity:

- Low for historical calculation
- High for forward-looking estimation
- Very high for optimization purposes

2.2.4. Lower Partial Moments

Lower partial moments (LPM), introduced by Fishburn (1977), provide a flexible framework for measuring the downside risk relative to a target return. The general form is as follows:

$$LPM_n(\tau) = E[\max(0, \tau - R_P)^n] \quad (7)$$

where τ is the investor's benchmark return level and n is the moment order:

n = 0: Probability-based risk measure.

n = 1: Measures the expected downside loss (used in the Sortino ratio).

n = 2: Captures the risk similarly to the variance, but only for negative deviations.

A common application of LPM is the Sortino ratio (Kaplan & Knowles, 2004), which is defined as follows:

$$Sortino = \frac{E[R_P] - \tau}{\sqrt{LPM_2(\tau)}} \quad (8)$$

Unlike the Sharpe ratio, which penalizes both upside and downside volatility, the Sortino ratio focuses exclusively on downside deviations, making it a more intuitive risk measure for investors.

Advantages:

- Flexible framework for different risk preferences
- Directly incorporates target returns
- Theoretically sound for asymmetric distributions

Drawbacks:

- Parameter selection can be subjective
- Less intuitive than other measures
- Limited regulatory recognition

Computational complexity:

- Low for historical calculation
- Moderate for parametric approaches
- High for optimization implementation

2.2.5. Implementation Considerations

The practical implementation of the above risk measures requires careful consideration of the data requirements and computational resources. Modern risk management systems typically support VaR and CVaR calculations, while MDD and LPM may require custom implementation. As highlighted by Alexander (2008), the choice of risk measure should align with the investment objectives, regulatory requirements, and available computational resources.

Backtesting and model validation remain crucial aspects of risk measure implementation. Christoffersen (1998) developed formal frameworks for testing VaR models, while similar approaches have since been extended to other risk measures.

Data requirements:

- VaR: Minimum 250 daily observations recommended
- CVaR: Requires 2–3 times more data than the VaR
- MDD: Full price history needed
- LPM: Flexible, depends on the measurement frequency

Software and systems:

- VaR: Widely supported in risk management systems
- CVaR: Growing support in modern platforms
- MDD: Basic calculation in most systems
- LPM: Often requires custom implementation

Regulatory acceptance:

- VaR: Standard requirement of the Basel framework
- CVaR: Increasingly recognized by regulators
- MDD: Common in fund reporting
- LPM: Limited regulatory application

This comparative analysis demonstrates that each risk measure offers distinct advantages and faces specific challenges. The choice of measure should align with the investor's objectives, data availability, computational resources, and regulatory requirements. Many institutions employ multiple measures to gain a more comprehensive view of the portfolio risk.

2.3. Empirical Illustrations of Downside Risk Measures

This section presents empirical evidence demonstrating the practical applications and comparative behaviors of different downside risk measures across various market conditions and asset classes. Thus, the analysis provides concrete illustrations of how these measures capture different aspects of risk.

2.3.1. Historical vs. Parametric VaR Analysis

Consider a diversified portfolio consisting of major asset classes tracked over the period 2019–2024. Figure 1 illustrates the comparison between the historical and parametric VaR at a 95% confidence level, as computed using weekly returns.

The figure presents a comparative analysis of the historical and parametric VaR estimates for the Morgan Stanley Capital International (MSCI) All-Country World Index (ACWI), covering the period from 2019 to early 2024, with a particular emphasis on the COVID-19 market stress period. The analysis reveals several significant patterns in the risk measurement dynamics. The historical VaR (shown by the solid line) demonstrates a more discrete, step-like pattern, while the parametric VaR (represented by the dashed line) exhibits smoother transitions. This difference reflects the inherent methodological characteristics of each approach.

During the pre-pandemic period (2019), both the parametric and historical VaR methodologies showed remarkable convergence, typically varying by less than 0.25 percentage points. This alignment suggests that both approaches effectively capture the market risk during periods of relative stability.

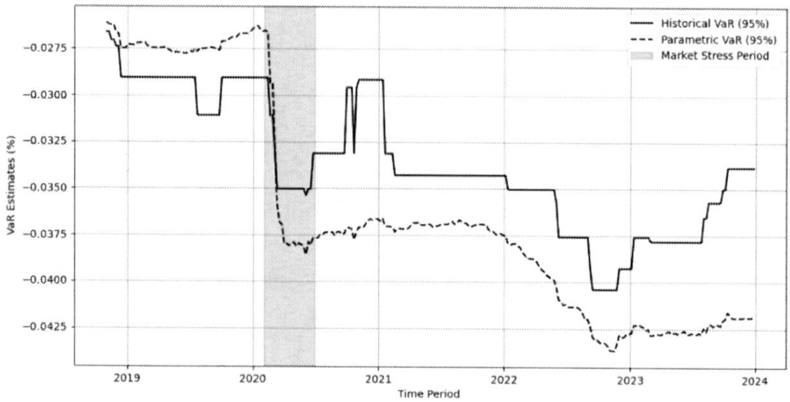

Source: Author's own illustration.

Figure 1. Comparison of Historical and Parametric VaR (95%).

Post-COVID-19 Evolution: In the post-COVID-19 recovery phase, both VaR measures gradually adapted to the new market conditions, albeit with different adjustment patterns:

1. The parametric VaR showed a gradual increase in the risk estimates, reaching approximately -4.25% by late 2022, suggesting a more conservative risk assessment.
2. The historical VaR maintained more stable levels of around -3.50%, with occasional adjustments reflecting the rolling window's composition.

The divergence between the two measures, which is particularly evident in the latter part of the observation period, highlights the importance of considering multiple risk measurement approaches. The parametric VaR's consistently higher risk estimates in recent periods suggest that it may be capturing structural changes in market volatility that the historical approach's discrete nature might not fully reflect. These findings reinforce the importance of employing multiple risk measurement approaches, as recommended by Alexander (2008), particularly during periods of market stress, when traditional assumptions regarding return distributions may not hold. This analysis underscores the complementary nature of the parametric and historical VaR methodologies in providing a comprehensive view of the market risk.

2.3.2. Lower Partial Moments and Sortino Ratio Analysis

Traditional risk measures, such as variance and the standard deviation, often fail to capture the asymmetric nature of the downside risk in financial markets. LPMs and the Sortino ratio provide alternative frameworks that focus solely on negative deviations from a target return, making them more suitable for assessing the downside risk in emerging and developed markets.

We calculate the LPM(0), LPM(1), and LPM(2) for the MSCI Emerging Markets (EM) and MSCI World indices using a target return (τ) of zero. Additionally, we compute the Sortino ratio to evaluate the risk-adjusted performance of the two indices. The analysis is conducted using daily data from the past five years (2020–2024) to ensure a comprehensive assessment of the downside risk trends. The following table summarizes the LPM and Sortino ratio calculations for both indices.

Table 2. LPM and Sortino Ratio Analysis of Global Market Indices

Metric	MSCI World	MSCI EM
LPM(0)	1.0	1.0
LPM(1)	0.0035	0.0039
LPM(2)	0.000068	0.000064
Sortino Ratio	0.04999	0.00414

The results reveal several important insights concerning the downside risk characteristics of developed and emerging markets. MSCI EM exhibits a slightly higher LPM(1) value (0.0039) when compared with MSCI World (0.0035), indicating that emerging markets tend to experience deeper losses when returns fall below the target threshold. This aligns with the general understanding that emerging markets are more susceptible to significant downside movements during periods of market stress.

However, the LPM(2) values show an interesting pattern, with MSCI World demonstrating a marginally higher value (0.000068) than MSCI EM (0.000064). This suggests that while emerging markets may experience more frequent downside deviations, the severity of these deviations in developed markets, when they do occur, can be more pronounced.

The Sortino ratio calculations provide particularly telling insights. MSCI World's Sortino ratio (0.04999) substantially exceeds that of MSCI EM

(0.00414), suggesting that developed markets offer better risk-adjusted returns when considering only downside volatility. This significant difference indicates that investors in developed markets are better compensated for the downside risk they assume.

3. Optimal Risky Portfolios

The advances in risk measurement techniques discussed in the previous section naturally led to their application in portfolio optimization. While traditional portfolio theory, as pioneered by Markowitz (1952), revolutionized investment management through mean–variance optimization, modern portfolio construction has evolved to incorporate more sophisticated risk measures that better reflect both investor preferences and market realities.

Recent research has shown that portfolios that are optimized using downside risk measures often provide superior protection during periods of market stress while maintaining competitive returns under normal market conditions (Kettunen & Salo, 2017; Yue et al. 2018; Landsman et al. 2022). This section explores how the VaR, CVaR, and drawdown constraints can be incorporated into portfolio optimization frameworks to create more robust investment strategies.

The key innovation of modern risk-based portfolio optimization lies in addressing several limitations of traditional mean–variance optimization (MVO). First, by focusing on downside risk rather than symmetric volatility, these approaches better align with investor preferences for loss aversion, as documented in the behavioral finance literature (Kahneman & Tversky, 1979; Benartzi & Thaler, 1995; Barberis et al. 2001). Second, they can capture the non-normal return distributions and tail risks that have become increasingly relevant in modern financial markets. Third, they provide more intuitive risk constraints that directly connect to institutional investment policies and regulatory requirements.

This section proceeds as follows. First, we examine minimum VaR portfolios, including both parametric and non-parametric optimization approaches. Next, we explore minimum CVaR optimization, which offers advantages in terms of the mathematical properties and computational implementation. Finally, we investigate optimal drawdown portfolios, which are particularly relevant for investment managers with explicit drawdown constraints. Throughout this section, we emphasize both the theoretical foundations and the practical implementation considerations, recognizing that the computational complexity and data requirements often influence the choice of optimization approach in real-world applications.

3.1. The Evolution of Portfolio Risk Optimization

The evolution of portfolio optimization from traditional mean–variance approaches to modern risk-based methods represents a fundamental shift in investment management. While Markowitz's (1952) MVO established the foundation for quantitative portfolio management, contemporary approaches increasingly incorporate downside risk measures to better reflect real-world market dynamics and investor preferences.

The classical MVO problem can be formulated as follows:

$$\min_{w} w^T \Sigma w \tag{9}$$

$$\text{subject to: } w^T \mu = r_t, \sum w_i = 1, w_i \geq 0 \tag{10}$$

where w is the vector of the portfolio weights, Σ is the covariance matrix of the asset returns, μ is the expected return vector, and r_t is the target portfolio return.

Despite its theoretical appeal, MVO has several practical limitations:

1. Symmetric risk treatment: MVO penalizes both upside and downside deviations equally, which does not align with investor behavior (Kahneman & Tversky, 1979).
2. Normality assumption: Real-world returns exhibit both fat tails and negative skewness, violating the normality assumption underlying variance-based risk models (Mandelbrot, 1963; Fama, 1965).
3. Instability in estimations: The covariance matrix can be highly sensitive to estimation errors, leading to unstable portfolio weights (Merton, 1980).

These limitations have led to the development of alternative portfolio optimization methods that explicitly account for asymmetric risk, tail events, and extreme losses.

3.2. Minimum VaR Portfolio

The minimum VaR (Min-VaR) portfolio is a portfolio optimization approach that minimizes the VaR, which measures the potential maximum loss over a specified time horizon at a given confidence level. Unlike traditional MVO, the Min-VaR portfolio explicitly focuses on reducing extreme losses, making it particularly relevant for investors and financial institutions concerned about the downside risk.

The Min-VaR portfolio aims to minimize the portfolio VaR while ensuring a target return:

$$\min_{w} VaR_{\alpha}(w) \tag{11}$$

$$\text{subject to: } w^T \mu = r_t, \sum w_i = 1, w_i \geq 0 \tag{12}$$

where w is the vector of the portfolio weights, μ is the expected return vector, and r_t is the target portfolio return. Moreover, $\sum w_i = 1$ ensures full capital allocation.

Several techniques exist for solving the Min-VaR optimization problem:

1. Quadratic Programming for the Parametric VaR

If returns are normally distributed, the Min-VaR optimization simplifies to a quadratic programming problem, which is solvable using Markowitz's (1952, 1959) framework:

$$\min_{w} (w^T \Sigma w)^{1/2} - Z_{\alpha} \cdot (w^T \mu) \tag{13}$$

In Equation 13, $\min_{w}$ is the minimization operator with respect to w, w^T is the transpose of vector w, and Σ is the covariance matrix. Moreover, μ refers to the expected return vector, while Z_{α} is the Z-score at an alpha confidence level.

2. Linear Programming for the Historical Simulation-Based VaR

If the historical VaR is used, the optimization problem can be linearized as follows:

$$\min_{w} \text{Quantile}_{(1-\alpha)} - w^T R_t \tag{14}$$

In Equation 14, $\min_{w}$ is the minimization operator with respect to w. $\text{Quantile}_{(1-\alpha)}$ refers to the quantile at the (1-α) level and R_t is the historical returns matrix.

3. Monte-Carlo-Based Stochastic Optimization

For non-normal and non-linear cases, genetic algorithms (GAs), particle swarm optimization (PSO), or simulated annealing are used to approximate the optimal Min-VaR portfolio.

The Min-VaR portfolio offers a structured approach to downside risk minimization, although it has the following limitations:

- Fails to capture losses beyond the VaR threshold.
- Not a coherent risk measure (violates subadditivity).
- More sensitive to estimation errors when compared with variance.

For better risk-adjusted optimization, the minimum CVaR portfolio (as discussed in Section 3.3.) is often preferred, as it accounts for the tail risk beyond the VaR.

3.3. Minimum CVaR Portfolio

The CVaR, also known as the ES, is an advanced risk measure that estimates the expected loss beyond the VaR threshold. Unlike the VaR, which only provides a single quantile estimate, the CVaR accounts for the entire tail of the loss distribution, making it a more robust and coherent risk measure.

The growing recognition of the CVaR's theoretical advantages over the VaR has led to increased interest in CVaR-based portfolio optimization. Minimizing the CVaR in portfolio optimization ensures that the worst-case losses are managed more effectively, which is crucial for institutional investors, hedge funds, and regulatory risk management (Bertsimas et al. 2018).

The minimum CVaR (Min-CVaR) portfolio optimization problem can be formulated as follows:

$$\min_{w} CVaR_{\alpha}(w^T R) \tag{15}$$

$$\text{subject to: } w^T \mu \geq r_{target}, w^T 1 = 1, w_i \geq 0, \quad i = 1, \dots, n \tag{16}$$

Following the approach in Rockafellar and Uryasev's (2000) seminal work, CVaR optimization can be reduced to a linear programming problem:

$$\min_{w} v + \frac{1}{1-\alpha} E[(-w^T R - v)^+] \tag{17}$$

$$\text{subject to: } w^T \mu \geq r_{target}, w^T 1 = 1, w_i \geq 0, \quad i = 1, \dots, n \tag{18}$$

where v represents the VaR at the confidence level α and $(x)^+ = \max(0, x)$ denotes the positive part function.

Several computational methods exist for solving the Min-CVaR portfolio optimization problem:

1. Linear Programming (LP) Method
   - Based on Rockafellar and Uryasev (2000).
   - Converts the non-smooth CVaR function into a linear optimization problem.
   - Efficiently solvable using simplex or interior-point methods.
2. Monte Carlo Simulation
   - Simulates thousands of return scenarios and evaluates the CVaR empirically.
   - Works well for complex, non-normal distributions.
3. Machine-Learning-Based Optimization
   - Neural networks and reinforcement learning can optimize CVaR-based portfolios dynamically.
   - Useful for real-time risk management.

3.4. Comparison of Min-CVaR vs. Min-VaR Portfolios

The comparison between the Min-CVaR and Min-VaR portfolios reveals fundamental differences in their characteristics, implementation approaches, and practical applications. Min-VaR portfolios focus on measuring the potential losses at a specific confidence level, typically 95% or 99%. However, this approach has a significant limitation—namely, it only considers the threshold of potential losses, without accounting for their magnitude beyond that point. In contrast, Min-CVaR portfolios address this limitation by measuring the expected loss beyond the VaR threshold, thereby providing a more comprehensive view of the tail risk.

A crucial distinction lies in their mathematical properties. The CVaR satisfies all four axioms of coherent risk measures defined by Artzner et al. (1999): monotonicity, translation invariance, homogeneity, and most importantly, subadditivity. The VaR, however, fails to satisfy the subadditivity property, which means that the VaR of a combined portfolio can be greater than the sum of the individual VaRs. This lack of coherence in terms of the VaR can lead to suboptimal diversification decisions.

The optimization frameworks for these portfolios differ significantly:

Min-VaR Portfolio:

- Requires quadratic programming techniques when using parametric approaches.
- Often leads to non-convex optimization problems.
- May have multiple local minima, making global optimization challenging.
- Computationally more intensive for large portfolios.

Min-CVaR Portfolio:

- Can be reduced to LP problems.
- Results in convex optimization problems.
- Guarantees global optimal solutions.
- More computationally efficient and scalable.

Figure 2 shows the distribution of portfolio returns, with two key risk measures highlighted—that is, the VaR at the 95% confidence level (shown by the dashed vertical line) and the CVaR at the 95% confidence level (shown by the solid vertical line). The graph offers several important insights into the risk characteristics of these portfolios.

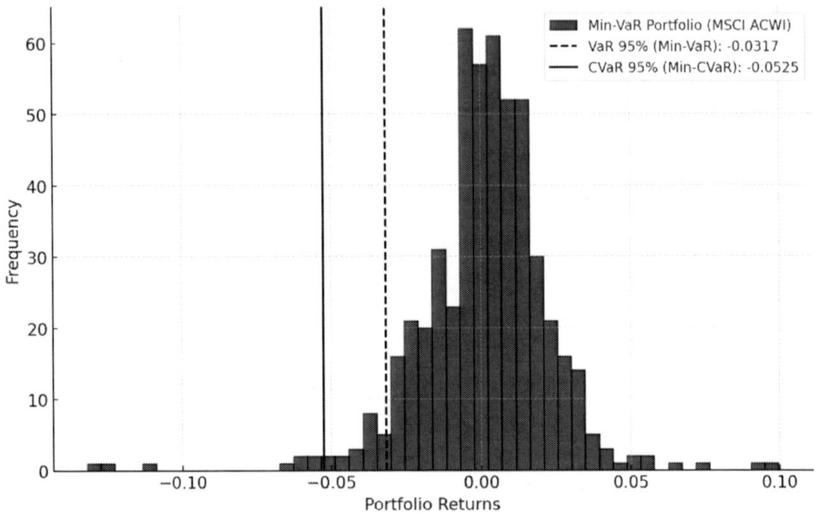

Source: Author's own illustration.

Figure 2. Min-VaR and Min-CVaR Portfolio Comparison for MSCI ACWI.

The return distribution exhibits slight negative skewness, with a longer left tail indicating a greater downside risk. The VaR measure at 95% confidence (-0.0317 or -3.17%) represents the threshold of potential losses in normal market conditions. However, the CVaR measure (-0.0525 or -5.25%) provides a more conservative risk assessment by capturing the average of losses beyond the VaR threshold. The difference between the VaR and CVaR values (approximately 208 basis points) highlights the significance of the tail risk in the MSCI ACWI portfolio. This substantial gap suggests that when extreme market events occur, the losses can be considerably larger than the VaR measure alone would indicate. The distribution's shape around these risk measures is particularly telling. While the majority of returns cluster around the mean, there is a notable frequency of returns in the left tail beyond the VaR threshold. This pattern validates the importance of using the CVaR as a risk measure, as it accounts for these more extreme negative outcomes, which the VaR might underestimate.

Research has shown that Min-CVaR portfolios consistently demonstrate superior performance during periods of market stress (Andersson et al. 2001; Rockafellar & Uryasev, 2002). This superiority stems from three key factors:

1. Better tail risk management: The CVaR's ability to capture the magnitude of extreme losses leads to more conservative portfolio allocations in terms of potentially risky assets.
2. Stable risk-adjusted allocation: The subadditivity property ensures that the diversification benefits are properly captured, resulting in more stable portfolio weights.
3. Risk control effectiveness: The CVaR's focus on the entire tail of the loss distribution, rather than on just a threshold, provides more comprehensive downside protection.

The choice between the Min-VaR and Min-CVaR portfolios ultimately depends on the investor's objectives, regulatory requirements, and risk management capabilities. However, the theoretical advantages and empirical evidence strongly support the use of Min-CVaR portfolios for comprehensive risk management in modern investment practice.

3.5. Optimal Drawdown Portfolios

The optimization of portfolio drawdown represents a critical advancement in relation to risk management, which is particularly relevant for institutional investors and fund managers who must maintain specific drawdown constraints. Unlike the VaR and CVaR, which focus on periodic returns, drawdown-based optimization directly addresses the path-dependent nature of investment performance and better aligns with investors' experience of portfolio risk.

Traditional risk measures focus on snapshot assessments of the risk at given time intervals, although they fail to capture the path-dependent nature of losses. Drawdowns, however, measure the peak-to-trough decline in portfolio value over time, offering a more dynamic perspective on the financial risk.

The most commonly used drawdown metrics include the following:

- *MDD:* The largest observed peak-to-trough decline within a specified period.
- *Average drawdown (ADD):* The mean of all the drawdowns occurring in a given timeframe.

- *Conditional drawdown at risk (CDaR):* A risk measure similar to the CVaR, which calculates the average of the worst drawdowns beyond a specified confidence level.
- *Ulcer index (UI):* A measure incorporating both the depth and the duration of drawdowns.

Among these, the CDaR has gained popularity in terms of portfolio optimization due to its ability to address the tail risks associated with prolonged losses. The optimization problem for an optimal drawdown portfolio seeks to minimize a drawdown-based risk metric while achieving a target level of expected return.

(a) Minimum Maximum Drawdown (Min-MDD) Portfolio:

A portfolio that minimizes the MDD is formulated as follows:

$$\min_{w} \max_{t \in [0,T]} D\,(t) \tag{19}$$

$$\text{subject to: } w^T \mu \geq r_{target}, w^T 1 = 1, w_i \geq 0, \quad i = 1, \ldots, n \tag{20}$$

As D(t) is a non-convex function, solving the Min-MDD optimization problem often requires dynamic programming or heuristic algorithms such as GAs and PSO.

(b) CDaR Optimization

Chekhlov et al. (2005) introduced the CDaR framework, which provides a more tractable approach to drawdown optimization. The CDaR, similar to the CVaR, provides a coherent measure of the drawdown risk by capturing extreme drawdown events beyond a certain quantile α. The optimization problem for a minimum CDaR (Min-CDaR) portfolio is formulated as follows:

$$\min_{w} E[\,D(t) \mid D(t) \geq D_\alpha\,] \tag{21}$$

$$\text{subject to: } w^T \mu \geq r_{target}, w^T 1 = 1, w_i \geq 0, \quad i = 1, \ldots, n \tag{22}$$

where D_α represents the drawdown threshold at the confidence level α.

Empirical research has shown that drawdown-constrained portfolios exhibit lower volatility and superior performance stability during financial crises (Yu, 2013; Alamdari et al. 2024). The benefits of incorporating drawdown constraints include the following:

- Improved risk-adjusted returns: Min-CDaR portfolios often achieve higher Sharpe and Sortino ratios when compared with traditional mean–variance portfolios.
- Robustness during market crises: Historical studies (e.g., 2008 global financial crisis, COVID-19 market crash) reveal that drawdown-optimized portfolios significantly outperform standard risk-based portfolios.
- Suitability for institutional investors: Pension funds and endowments prefer drawdown-based strategies due to their capital preservation features.

Recent research has extended the drawdown optimization framework to incorporate dynamic strategies and options-based tail risk hedging. For instance, Goldberg and Mahmoud (2017) demonstrated that combining drawdown optimization with dynamic allocation rules can improve performance during periods of market stress while maintaining competitive returns under normal market conditions.

The effectiveness of drawdown-optimized portfolios ultimately depends on the investment horizon and objectives. These portfolios typically demonstrate superior performance for longer-term investors who prioritize capital preservation and are particularly concerned about avoiding sustained losses. However, they may underperform in strong bull markets due to their inherently defensive positioning.

3.6. Hybrid Risk Optimization Approaches

In modern portfolio management, hybrid approaches that combine multiple risk measures have gained increasing importance when compared with single-measure optimization. Alexander and Baptista (2004) proposed a portfolio optimization model combining the VaR and CVaR constraints. Through an empirical analysis using data from the S&P 500 index, they demonstrated that this hybrid approach generated more stable portfolios than using either the VaR or CVaR alone.

Krokhmal et al. (2002) developed a multi-objective optimization model that integrates volatility and the CVaR. Their research revealed that combining these two risk measures improved portfolio performance, particularly during periods of market stress. They formulated the problem as follows:

$$\min_{w} \{\lambda \cdot \sigma^2(w) + (1-\lambda) \cdot CVaR_{\alpha}(w)\} \tag{23}$$

where $\lambda \in [0,1]$ represents the weight between risk measures.

Favre and Galeano (2002) introduced a comprehensive risk model for hedge funds that combines skewness, kurtosis, and the CVaR. Their hybrid approach successfully identified asymmetric risks that traditional risk measures failed to capture. Biglova et al. (2004) developed an optimization framework that incorporates four distinct risk measures (volatility, the VaR, the CVaR, and drawdown):

$$\min_{w} \left\{\alpha_1 \sigma(w) + \alpha_2 VaR_{\beta}(w) + \alpha_3 CVaR_{\gamma}(w) + \alpha_4 CDaR_{\delta}(w)\right\} \tag{24}$$

where the α_i values represent the relative weights between risk measures. More recently, Boudt et al. (2013) proposed a dynamic portfolio optimization model that combines the drawdown and CVaR constraints. Their model was formulated as follows:

$$\min_{w} \{CVaR_{\alpha}(w)\} \tag{25}$$

$$\text{subject to: } CDaR_{\beta}(w) \leq L \tag{26}$$

where L represents the maximum acceptable drawdown level.

Additionally, Li and Xu (2009) developed a novel approach to optimizing hybrid risk measures using machine learning techniques. The methodology employs deep learning models to dynamically determine the optimal weights between risk measures, demonstrating superior results when compared with traditional methods. These studies collectively demonstrate that hybrid risk optimization approaches provide more comprehensive and effective solutions than single-measure models. The prior research particularly highlights their enhanced reliability in terms of portfolio optimization during periods of market stress and scenarios involving asymmetric risk distributions.

4. Review of Current Applications

The theoretical frameworks and methodologies discussed in the preceding sections have found widespread practical applications across various segments of the investment management industry. This section examines how different types of institutions implement these risk measurement and portfolio optimization approaches, highlighting both the successes and challenges in real-world applications.

4.1. Institutional Implementation

Large financial institutions have increasingly adopted sophisticated risk measurement frameworks that combine multiple approaches. Investment banks typically employ a hybrid model that integrates the VaR for regulatory reporting, the CVaR for internal risk assessment, and drawdown analysis for client communication. In particular, the Basel III framework has influenced how banks implement these measures, requiring them to maintain robust risk management systems that can capture both normal market conditions and stress scenarios.

Asset management firms have adapted the discussed risk frameworks to suit their specific investment mandates. For example, pension funds tend to emphasize drawdown control and long-term risk management, often implementing optimal drawdown portfolios with CVaR constraints. By contrast, hedge funds frequently employ more dynamic approaches, combining traditional risk measures with high-frequency monitoring and adaptive risk allocation strategies.

Insurance companies implement MDD- and CVaR-based models to optimize their risk exposure and prevent excessive portfolio losses. Hedge funds and investment funds adopt risk-sensitive optimization techniques to construct Min-CVaR portfolios or drawdown-controlled strategies that aim to minimize volatility while maintaining long-term sustainability. Moreover, private equity firms and pension funds leverage Monte Carlo simulations and machine-learning-based risk analytics to develop more dynamic portfolio management approaches.

4.2. Technological Integration

Advances in computing power and data analytics have transformed how institutions implement risk management systems. Cloud computing platforms now enable real-time risk calculations across large portfolios, while machine learning algorithms help identify emerging risk patterns and potential market stress scenarios. Modern portfolio management systems routinely incorporate multiple risk measures, allowing portfolio managers to view their exposure through different risk lenses simultaneously.

Machine learning applications have been particularly successful in enhancing the accuracy of risk measurement. Neural networks have shown promising results in predicting tail risk events, while reinforcement learning algorithms have improved the dynamic rebalancing of risk-optimized portfolios. These technological advances have made sophisticated risk management approaches more accessible to smaller institutions and wealth management firms.

4.3. Regulatory Framework and Compliance

The regulatory landscape has significantly influenced how different institutions implement risk measurement systems. The shift from the VaR to the CVaR in terms of the Basel III requirements reflects growing recognition of the importance of tail risk measurement. Financial institutions must now maintain more comprehensive risk monitoring systems that can demonstrate compliance with multiple regulatory standards while supporting the achievement of internal risk management objectives.

4.4. Practical Challenges and Solutions

Despite the theoretical advances, practitioners still face challenges when it comes to implementing risk measurement approaches:

- *Data quality and availability*: Historical data may not adequately capture current market conditions, particularly for new financial instruments or emerging markets. Institutions have responded to this challenge by developing synthetic data generation techniques and incorporating alternative data sources.
- *Computational complexity*: Real-time risk calculation for large portfolios remains computationally intensive. Advanced optimization techniques and distributed computing systems have helped address this challenge, although continued innovation is needed.
- *Model risk*: The reliance on complex mathematical models introduces model risk, particularly during periods of market stress. Thus, leading institutions have developed model validation frameworks that combine quantitative testing with qualitative oversight.

5. Conclusion and Future Outlook

5.1. Summary of Key Insights

This chapter has introduced a range of downside risk measures—the VaR, the CVaR, drawdown-based metrics, and LPM—and explored how each of them can be integrated into portfolio construction and optimization. We began the chapter by examining the historical development of these measures (Section 2), underscoring the limitations of variance-based approaches in capturing both asymmetric losses and tail events. We then demonstrated (Section 3) how modern portfolio optimization techniques incorporate these risk measures, offering more robust strategies that better align with investors' risk preferences and regulatory requirements. Finally, we reviewed (Section 4) the real-world implementations across various institutional settings, highlighting the practical considerations and challenges.

Based on the analysis in this chapter, the following overarching insights emerge:

1. Importance of Tail Events

- Traditional variance–covariance methods often underestimate the probability of extreme losses. Measures such as the CVaR and drawdown constraints provide a more nuanced view of the tail risk and help mitigate severe downside losses.

2. Behavioral and Regulatory Alignment
- Investors tend to be loss averse, as noted in the behavioral finance literature (Kahneman & Tversky, 1979; Benartzi & Thaler, 1995; Barberis et al. 2001). Downside-focused risk measures, particularly the CVaR and drawdown-based metrics, resonate well with this mindset. Moreover, regulatory shifts (e.g., Basel III) increasingly encourage institutions to adopt risk measures that account for fat-tailed distributions, further validating these approaches.

3. Dynamic and Data-Driven Approaches
- Advances in computing power and the growing sophistication of data science allow for more accurate modeling of complex market behaviors. Methods such as Monte Carlo simulation, machine learning, and advanced optimization algorithms are now central to the practical implementation of downside risk measurement techniques.

4. Diversification and Risk Aggregation
- Traditional mean–variance optimization may lead to highly concentrated or unstable portfolios under certain market conditions. Downside risk optimization fosters better risk aggregation, improving the balance between capital preservation and return-seeking behavior.

5.2. Implementation Challenges

Despite the clear advantages of downside risk measures and their integration into portfolio optimization, practitioners face the following notable hurdles:

1. Model Risk
- The VaR, the CVaR, and drawdown-based models rely on historical data or assumptions regarding return distributions that may not hold in future market regimes. Hence, institutions must conduct rigorous model validation and stress testing to mitigate the risk of model miscalibration.

2. Computational Complexity
- Although LP techniques for the CVaR and efficient heuristics for drawdown-based optimization exist, real-world portfolios consisting of thousands of instruments can still pose a computational burden. Efficient algorithms, cloud computing, and parallelization have helped, but they do not fully eliminate these challenges.

3. Data Quality and Frequency
- The accuracy of tail risk estimates depends heavily on the scope and granularity of the available data. Emerging markets, alternative investments, and rapidly evolving assets (e.g., cryptocurrencies) often lack a long history of reliable data, leading to potential estimation errors and biases.

4. Operational Integration
- Incorporating new risk measures into existing portfolio management workflows requires changes to the technology infrastructure, risk reporting processes, and staff training. Resistance to adopting novel metrics can also stem from organizational inertia or limited familiarity with advanced risk methodologies.

5.3. Future Directions

1. ESG and Climate Risk Integration
   - As sustainability considerations grow, institutions are incorporating environmental, social, and governance (ESG) factors into risk assessment. There is increasing interest in developing downside-focused methodologies that capture climate-related drawdowns and potential tail events triggered by regulatory or societal shifts.
2. Machine Learning and AI
   - Continued improvements in machine learning techniques (e.g., deep learning, reinforcement learning) will likely further enhance the accuracy and adaptability of downside risk measures. Dynamic portfolio rebalancing strategies that factor in real-time market signals, big data analytics, and alternative data may provide a competitive edge in risk management.
3. Scenario Analysis and Stress Testing
   - Scenario-based approaches that incorporate geopolitical events, macroeconomic shocks, or extreme climate events will become increasingly essential. Combining these scenarios with CVaR or drawdown optimization can help investors design robust portfolios that perform reasonably well even under highly adverse conditions.

4. Expansion to Digital Assets and Non-Traditional Markets
    - The rapid growth of digital assets (cryptocurrencies, tokenized securities) and alternative investments (private equity, crowdfunding platforms) poses new challenges to traditional risk frameworks. Tailoring downside metrics for assets with limited historical data or exhibiting higher volatility and illiquidity will be a focal point of future research.
5. Enhanced Regulatory and Industry Collaboration
    - Regulatory requirements are evolving toward more comprehensive, tail-oriented risk measures. Collaboration between regulators, industry practitioners, and academic researchers can drive methodological improvements and standardize best practices for risk management.

References

Acerbi, C., & Tasche, D. (2002). Expected Shortfall: A Natural Coherent Alternative to Value at Risk. *Economic Notes*, *31*(2), 379–388.

Alamdari, M. K., Esfahanipour, A., & Dastkhan, H. (2024). A Portfolio Trading System using a Novel Pixel Graph Network for Stock Selection and a Mean-CDaR Optimization for Portfolio Rebalancing. *Applied Soft Computing*, *152*, 111213. https://doi.org/10.1016/j.asoc.2023.111213.

Alexander, C. (2008). *Market Risk Analysis, Quantitative Methods in Finance*. John Wiley & Sons.

Alexander, G. J., & Baptista, A. M. (2004). A Comparison of VaR and CVaR Constraints on Portfolio Selection with the Mean-Variance Model. *Management Science*, *50*(9), 1261–1273.

Andersson, F., Mausser, H., Rosen, D., & Uryasev, S. (2001). Credit Risk Optimization with Conditional Value-at-Risk Criterion. *Mathematical Programming*, *89*, 273–291. https://doi.org/10.1007/PL00011399.

Artzner, P., Delbaen, F., Eber, J. M., & Heath, D. (1999). Coherent Measures of Risk. *Mathematical Finance*, *9*(3), 203–228.

Barberis, N., Huang, M., & Santos, T. (2001). Prospect Theory and Asset Prices. *The Quarterly Journal of Economics*, *116*(1), 1–53. https://doi.org/10.1162/003355301556310.

Benartzi, S., & Thaler, R. H. (1995). Myopic Loss Aversion and the Equity Premium Puzzle. *The Quarterly Journal of Economics*, *110*(1), 73–92. https://doi.org/10.2307/2118511.

Bertsimas, D., Gupta, V., & Kallus, N. (2018). Data-Driven Robust Optimization. *Mathematical Programming*, *167*, 235–292.

Biglova, A., Ortobelli, S., Rachev, S. T., & Stoyanov, S. (2004). Different Approaches to Risk Estimation in Portfolio Theory. *The Journal of Portfolio Management*, *31*(1), 103–112.

Boudt, K., Carl, P., & Peterson, B. G. (2013). Asset Allocation with Conditional Value-at-Risk Budgets. *Journal of Risk*, *15*(3), 39–68.

Cont, R. (2010). *Encyclopedia of Quantitative Finance* (Vol. 1). John Wiley & Sons.

Chekhlov, A., Uryasev, S., & Zabarankin, M. (2005). Drawdown Measure in Portfolio Optimization. *International Journal of Theoretical and Applied Finance*, *8*(01), 13–58.

Christoffersen, P. F. (1998). Evaluating Interval Forecasts. *International Economic Review*, *39*(4), 841–862.

Danielsson, J., & De Vries, C. G. (2000). Value-at-Risk and Extreme Returns. *Annales d'Économie et de Statistique*, *60*, 239–270. https://doi.org/10.2307/20076262.

Duffie, D., & Pan, J. (1997). An Overview of Value at Risk. *Journal of Derivatives*, *4*(3), 7–49.

Engle, R. (2002). Dynamic Conditional Correlation: A Simple Class of Multivariate Generalized Autoregressive Conditional Heteroskedasticity Models. *Journal of Business & Economic Statistics*, *20*(3), 339–350.

Fama, E. F. (1965). The Behavior of Stock-Market Prices. *The Journal of Business*, *38*(1), 34–105.

Favre, L., & Galeano, J. A. (2002). Mean-Modified Value-at-Risk Optimization with Hedge Funds. *The Journal of Alternative Investments*, *5*(2), 21–25.

Fishburn, P. C. (1977). Mean-Risk Analysis with Risk Associated with Below-Target Returns. *The American Economic Review*, *67*(2), 116–126.

Glasserman, P. (2003). *Monte Carlo Methods in Financial Engineering*. Springer.

Goldberg, L. R., & Mahmoud, O. (2017). Drawdown: From Practice to Theory and Back Again. *Mathematics and Financial Economics*, *11*, 275–297.

Grossman, S. J., & Zhou, Z. (1993). Optimal Investment Strategies for Controlling Drawdowns. *Mathematical Finance*, *3*(3), 241–276. https://doi.org/10.1111/j.1467-9965.1993.tb00044.x.

Jorion, P. (2007). *Value at Risk: The New Benchmark for Managing Financial Risk* (3rd ed.). McGraw-Hill.

Kahneman, D., & Tversky, A. (1979). Prospect Theory: An Analysis of Decision under Risk. *Econometrica*, *47*(2), 263–291.

Kaplan, P. D., & Knowles, J. A. (2004). Kappa: A Generalized Downside Risk-Adjusted Performance Measure. *Journal of Performance Measurement*, *8*, 42-54.

Kettunen, J., & Salo, A. (2017). Estimation of Downside Risks in Project Portfolio Selection. *Production and Operations Management*, *26*(10), 1839–1853. https://doi.org/10.1111/poms.12727.

Krokhmal, P., Palmquist, J., & Uryasev, S. (2002). Portfolio Optimization with Conditional Value-at-Risk Objective and Constraints. *Journal of Risk*, *4*, 43–68.

Landsman, Z., Makov, U., Yao, J., & Zhou, M. (2022). Downside Risk Optimization with Random Targets and Portfolio Amplitude. *The European Journal of Finance*, *28*(16), 1642–1663. https://doi.org/10.1080/1351847X.2021.1991421.

Li, J., & Xu, J. (2009). A Novel Portfolio Selection Model in a Hybrid Uncertain Environment. *Omega*, *37*(2), 439–449. https://doi.org/10.1016/j.omega.2007.06.002.

Mandelbrot, B. (1963). The Variation of Certain Speculative Prices. *The Journal of Business*, *36*(4), 394–419.

Markowitz, H. (1952). Portfolio Selection. *The Journal of Finance*, *7*(1), 77–91.

Markowitz, H. M. (1959). *Portfolio Selection: Efficient Diversification of Investments*. John Wiley & Sons.

McNeil, A. J., & Frey, R. (2000). Estimation of Tail-Related Risk Measures for Heteroscedastic Financial Time Series: An Extreme Value Approach. *Journal of Empirical Finance*, *7*(3-4), 271–300. https://doi.org/10.1016/S0927-5398(00)00012-8.

McNeil, A. J., Frey, R., & Embrechts, P. (2015). *Quantitative Risk Management: Concepts, Techniques and Tools* (2nd ed.). Princeton University Press.

Merton, R. C. (1980). On Estimating the Expected return on the Market: An Exploratory Investigation. *Journal of Financial Economics*, *8*(4), 323–361.

Rockafellar, R. T., & Uryasev, S. (2000). Optimization of Conditional Value-at-Risk. *Journal of Risk*, *2*, 21–42.

Rockafellar, R. T., & Uryasev, S. (2002). Conditional Value-at-Risk for General Loss Distributions. *Journal of Banking and Finance*, *26*(7), 1443–1471. https://doi.org/10.1016/S0378-4266(02)00271-6.

Roy, A. D. (1952). Safety First and the Holding of Assets. *Econometrica*, *20*(3), 431–449.

Yue, W., Wang, Y., & Xuan, H. (2018). Fuzzy Multi-Objective Portfolio Model Based on Semi-Variance–Semi-Absolute Deviation Risk Measures. *Soft Computing*, *23*, 8159–8179. https://doi.org/10.1007/s00500-018-3452-y.

Yu, X. (2013). The Optimal Robust Portfolio Model Based on CDaR. *Advanced Materials Research*, *756*, 2883–2886. https://doi.org/10.4028/www.scientific.net/AMR.756-759.2883.

Chapter 3

Behavioral Portfolio Management

Cemile Özgür[1,*], PhD and Vedat Sarikovanlik[2], PhD

[1]Department of Management Information Systems, Boğaziçi University, Istanbul, Türkiye
[2]Department of Finance, Istanbul University, Istanbul, Türkiye

Abstract

The first section of this chapter introduces the reader to *homo economicus*, the purely rational and self-interested agent who seeks to maximize only his/her utility in all situations. While the *economic man* of traditional economic theory might sound appealing, there is a growing body of literature on the deviations of observed human behavior from the behavior of this self-interested agent. Hence, the first section also discusses some of these behavioral gaps in terms of rational decision making and the violations of expected utility theory that are well documented and counted as cornerstones of the related literature. The second section is concerned with prospect theory, which was proposed by Kahneman and Tversky in 1979. This theory can be safely classified as one of the significant milestones in the field of economics, as it integrates some of the major psychological insights concerning humans into economic choice. The third and fourth sections briefly discuss two additional theories incorporating the psychological or behavioral traits of individuals into decision making under risk and uncertainty—namely, the security–potential/aspiration and behavioral portfolio theories that were proposed in 1987 and 2000, respectively. The fifth section then presents the experimental set up and reports the empirical results of a

* Corresponding Author's Email: cemile.ozgur@pt.bogazici.edu.tr / ozgurcemile@yahoo.com

In: Asset Allocation: Theory, Recent Developments and Beyond
Editors: Cemile Özgür and Vedat Sarikovanlik
ISBN: 979-8-89530-649-9

research study in which the portfolio choices of participants are obtained through laboratory experiments. The portfolio allocations of the participants are compared with the allocations of the tangency portfolio and the commonly employed equally weighted portfolio. Additionally, participants' portfolio choices are also predicted using a deep learning algorithm. Finally, the last section concludes this chapter by providing an overview of each preceding section.

Keywords: rational choice, prospect theory, behavioral portfolio theory, tangency portfolio, copula functions, deep learning

1. Behavioral Gaps Related to Rational Choice

According to traditional economic theory, an individual is assumed to be *homo economicus*. This model of the individual exhibits several behavioral characteristics. Principally, homo economicus or *economic man* is a purely rational and self-interested agent who seeks to maximize only his/her utility in all situations and transactions. As explained by Barnes (1988), the concept of homo economicus provides neoclassical economics with a methodological structure, which is based on the rational choice that enables the representation of individual behavior in a formal model by decreasing the complexity of economic situations. However, while the term "economic man" dates back to the time of Mill (1836), the adoption or definition of homo economicus in the neoclassical sense is more restrictive than the concept used in Mill's (1836) work (Urbina & Ruiz-Villaverde, 2019).

The behavioral characteristics of homo economicus can be summarized as follows. First, the pure rationality characteristic postulates that economic agents are fully rational individuals with the ability to objectively process all the available choices or decision variables without any cognitive bias. Second, the characteristics of individualism (self-interest) and behavior optimization indicate that agents are purely self-interested individuals who seek and act only in accordance with their interest by maximizing the utility they obtain (see Chapter 1 for the definition of utility). Agents can consider others' welfare if their own welfare is affected. In this sense, the behavior of economic individuals (agents) is grounded in a pure mathematical representation of a constrained optimization problem. Third, economic man has certain preferences. Economic theory assumes that agents base their decisions on the marginal utility obtained and have certain exogenous preferences. With the help of these preferences, agents can rank and decide on the alternative(s) yielding the maximum expected utility. In this context, individual preferences must meet certain assumptions, which are defined by the four axioms of *completeness*, *transitivity*, *continuity*, and *independence* (von Neumann & Morgenstern, 1944). These four axioms make it clear that one option is preferred to another only if the agent will obtain a higher expected utility. Fourth, universality refers to the validity of the characteristics of economic man in relation to all human behavior, independent of both society and time.

Nevertheless, it has been shown that the actual behavior of agents significantly deviates from the model of homo economicus. An early work by Allais (1953), the well-known *Allais Paradox*, showed that individuals violate the preference axioms when asked to choose between two specific lottery pairs. Tversky (1975) explained the underlying reason for this violation to be the *certainty effect*. As mentioned by Simon (1955:99), the traditional model of rational behavior includes the assumptions of knowledge about the full set of decision variables (e.g., all the decision-specific choices, the possible outcomes of those choices, and their probabilities of occurrence), well-organized preferences, and intellectual ability to process all the available information and make calculations. Unfortunately, at least some of these assumptions do not hold true in real-life decision-making processes. As a result, Simon (1955) proposed the model of *bounded rationality*, which explains the reasons for deviations from rational choice to be a consequence of limited knowledge regarding the set of decision variables and/or limited intellectual capacity to process all the information. Simon (1955) argued that individuals use different methods or simplifications that lead to bounded rational decision making. Among them are the classification of the outcomes of different choices/actions as being either "satisfactory" or "unsatisfactory" based on a minimum level of *aspiration* and an incomplete evaluation of all the possible decisions or actions and their outcomes by choosing the satisfactory one at the beginning. According to Simon (1955), individuals do not maximize their decision making but rather engage in *satisficing*, which defines the decisions that are made when a good enough or satisfactory alternative is identified without dedicating additional effort to searching for all the alternatives in order to identify the best one.

After Simon (1955), another cornerstone showing the behavioral violations of the axioms of preference was the work by Kahneman and Tversky (1979), which led to the development of *prospect theory* (see the next section for a detailed review of prospect theory). Moreover, one of the other implications of the concept of bounded rationality is that it opened the doors to further developments, such as *heuristics*. The term "heuristics" refers to the simplified process of individual thinking when faced with complex decisions. According to Gigerenzer and Gaissmaier (2011), the term has a Greek origin and a meaning of "serving to find out or discover." However, the term currently has a broader meaning that includes any type of shortcut used in making a decision for the purpose of rendering the decision-making process faster or decreasing the complexity of it (Wilkinson & Klaes, 2012).

Following Simon (1955) and Kahneman and Tversky (1979), the literature concerning the behavioral violations of the rational choice theory and/or axioms of preference has rapidly grown. The following sections discuss the main milestones in terms of the choice behavior of individuals under uncertainty—that is, prospect theory, security–potential/aspiration theory, and behavioral portfolio theory.

2. Prospect Theory

Prospect theory (PT) was proposed by Daniel Kahneman and Aaron Tversky in 1979. As part of the related work, Kahneman and Tversky (1979) examined the descriptive validity of expected utility theory (EUT) and its axioms by asking individuals (students and faculty members) several hypothetical choice-related questions consisting of risky and/or risk-free choices. Kahneman and Tversky (1979) analyzed the outcomes (individual choices) and identified several violations of EUT. One of these violations was the certainty effect (CE), which was used to explain the underlying reason for the Allais paradox. As defined by Kahneman and Tversky (1979), the CE refers to a phenomenon that describes an individual's behavior in overweighting certain outcomes when compared with merely probable outcomes. Moreover, the case of the Allais paradox is an example of a violation of the independence axiom of EUT.

Another violation of EUT identified by Kahneman and Tversky (1979) is the fact while the CE contributes to explaining the risk-averse preferences for choices without losses, the same effect (the CE) contributes to the risk-seeking preferences when the same choices are all associated with losses. In other words, when individuals are asked to make a choice between negative prospects, they prefer the one with a higher expected loss (a loss of $4,000) rather than the one with a lower and certain amount of loss (e.g., a loss of $3,000). Kahneman and Tversky (1979) referred to this observation as the *reflection effect*. The psychological trait of the *overweighting of certainty* results in a risk-averse behavior in terms of choices with gains. By contrast, the same trait favors risk-seeking behavior when the choices are related to the loss domain.

Furthermore, according to Kahneman and Tversky (1979), individuals ignore the common or shared components of alternative choices and make decisions based on the distinguishing components of the choices, which leads to inconsistent preferences within the rational choice framework. He termed this behavioral observation the *isolation effect*.

Following the identification of several behavioral violations of EUT, Kahneman and Tversky (1979) proposed a "subjective utility" $(V(.))$ function that can integrate the behavioral effects discussed in the previous paragraphs.

$$V(y, p;\ z, q) = v(y)\pi(p) + v(z)\pi(q) \tag{1}$$

where y and z represent the two non-zero outcomes of a choice, $v(.)$ refers to a value function defined based on the outcomes ($v(0) = 0$), and $\pi(.)$ is the *probability weighting function*, which yields the subjective probabilities for each outcome by assigning weights to the real probabilities ($\pi(0) = 0 \wedge \pi(1) = 1$). Moreover, $y \geq 0 \geq z$, or $p + q < 1$, or $z \geq 0 \geq y$.

Kahneman and Tversky (1979) suggested a slightly different version of Equation 1 for strictly negative ($y < z < 0$) or strictly positive ($y > z > 0$) outcomes with $p + q = 1$ as follows:

$$V(y, p;\ z, q) = v(z) + \pi(p)[v(y) - v(z)] \tag{2}$$

Equation 2 defines the subjective value of a prospect in terms of the value of its riskless part, the difference between the values of the outcomes, and the weight (subjective probability) of the relatively extreme outcome. Overall, it is possible to summarize the unique properties of PT that differentiate it from EUT as follows:

1. PT argues that individuals decide from among different alternatives relative to a point of reference and based on the effects of the corresponding choices measured in terms of changes in wealth.
2. PT assumes that individuals are risk averse when the wealth changes are associated with gains and risk seeking when the wealth changes arise from losses.

3. According to PT, individuals have non-linear preferences and tend to "overweight small probabilities" (Kahneman & Tversky, 1979), which leads to risk-seeking behavior for large gains or risk-averse behavior for losses even when the probability of occurrence is very small.
4. PT argues that individuals place more emphasis on losses than on gains. The observed aversion to losses, termed *loss aversion*, cannot simply be hidden behind the effects of different income levels or diminishing risk aversion.
5. EUT assumes that individuals are rational utility maximizers without any psychological biases; however, PT incorporates various psychological traits into individual decision making and emphasizes the importance of the *framing* of decision alternatives.

Later, Tversky and Kahneman (1992) proposed a different version of PT called *cumulative prospect theory* (CPT). CPT extends PT by using the cumulative probabilities (decision weights) in place of the separable ones and accounting for both uncertainty and risk. PT and the subsequent works by Daniel Kahneman and Amos Tversky provide major psychological insights into economic choice, thereby opening the doors to further behavioral research concerning rational decision making under risk and uncertainty. Daniel Kahneman was awarded the Nobel Prize in Economic Sciences in 2002 for his contributions to the field of economics, although much of his prize-related work was conducted with Amos Tversky.

3. Security–Potential/Aspiration Theory

Security–potential/aspiration (SP/A) theory was proposed by Lola Lopes, a psychologist, in a 1987 article titled "Beyond Hope and Fear: The Psychology of Risk." SP/A is an abstraction of its three main components—namely, "security" (fear), "potential" (hope), and "aspiration." Individual behavior has "inner" and "outer" sources, but it is the stimuli that evoke responses or alter them depending on the changing conditions (Mischel, 1968; Lopes, 1987). SP/A theory is based on two factors that are used to define the risky choices of individuals. The first factor is called *the dispositional factor* and refers to the motives that lead individuals to desire security (S) or exploit potential (P). Lopes (1987) used security-oriented motives to explain risk-averse behavior and potential-oriented motives to explain the risk-seeking behavior of individuals. The second factor is termed the *situational factor* and refers to individual responses to opportunities as well as the needs and constraints imposed by a situation or environment. The "A" in SP/A theory represents the situational factor of aspiration.

As explained by Lopes (1987), there are two sources of conflict in the theory. One is the trade-off between the desire for security (the fear component) and the desire to exploit potential (the hope component). Lopes (1987) continued by offering the risk and return trade-off in finance as an example, asserting that an individual needs to pay for the desired safety. The other source of conflict is associated with different situations that might result in different responses between security or potential and the opportunities and needs influencing the level of aspiration. More formally, SP/A theory defines the expected value of the wealth of individuals $\left(E_h(W)\right)$ as follows:

$$h(\mathcal{D}) = \delta h_s(\mathcal{D}) + (1-\delta)h_p(\mathcal{D}) \tag{3}$$

$$h(\mathcal{D}_{k+1}) - h(\mathcal{D}_k) \tag{4}$$

Equation 3 defines the expected wealth of an individual $\left(E(W)\right)$ in terms of a *decumulative distribution function* $(\mathcal{D})$ with the form of $\mathcal{D}(z) = Prob(W \geq z)$. The parameter δ refers to the strength of fear relative to that of hope. Moreover, h_s and h_p are the transformation functions of fear (security) and hope (potential), respectively. Equation 4 shows the replacement of $E(W)$ with $E_h(W)$ by substituting the probability attached to the kth event with their difference (Rengifo et al. 2014; Chen, 2016).

Lopes (1987) argued that risky choices are evaluated according to their expected value in terms of wealth $\left(E_h(W)\right)$ as well as the $\mathcal{D}(\mathcal{A})$. $\mathcal{D}(\mathcal{A})$ refers to the probability that an event (risky choice) will yield a payoff of $\mathcal{A}$ or higher. In other words, it is the probability of a risky choice yielding an outcome at or above an individual aspiration level. Overall, while SP/A theory is based on the safety-first principle, it is a behavioral model of risky choice that involves balancing the security, hope, and potential factors acting against the aspiration level. In addition, it can be seen as a general framework for portfolio choice under risk and uncertainty.

4. Behavioral Portfolio Theory

Behavioral portfolio theory (BPT) was proposed by Hersh Shefrin and Meir Statman in 2000. Shefrin and Statman (2000) developed BPT on the grounds of the two theories explained in the preceding sections—namely, PT and SP/A. BPT holds that individuals do not construct portfolios by looking at the mean and variance statistics of asset returns as defined in the mean–variance framework; instead, they evaluate the "expected wealth, desire for security and potential, aspiration levels, and probabilities of achieving aspiration levels." Thus, Shefrin and Statman (2000) argued that the optimal portfolios within the mean–variance framework differ from BPT.

Moreover, Shefrin and Statman (2000) proposed two different versions of BPT—that is, *single mental account* BPT (BPT-SA) and *multiple mental account* BPT (BPT-MA). BPT-SA portfolios are similar to the mean–variance approach in the sense that they both evaluate the portfolio as a whole (i.e., as a single account) by using covariances, although they differ in one key respect. The optimal mean–variance portfolios on the efficient frontier are obtained by either maximizing the portfolio return (μ) for a certain level of portfolio risk (σ) or minimizing the portfolio risk for a given level of return. By contrast, the optimal portfolios on the efficient frontier of BPT-SA are obtained by maximizing the expected value of wealth $\left(E_h(W)\right)$ for fixed $Prob(W \leq \mathcal{A})$. In their work, Shefrin and Statman (2000) showed that an efficient portfolio of BPT-SA is not an efficient portfolio on the mean–variance efficient frontier. Under the BPT-SA framework, individuals maximize $\mathcal{U}\left(E_h(W), \mathcal{D}(\mathcal{A})\right)$ along the efficient frontier of BPT-SA.

Furthermore, BPT-MA assumes that individuals overlook or ignore covariance information due to mental accounting. As a characteristic of PT, mental accounting leads to the segregation of portfolios into separate layers of mental accounts. Various aspiration levels contribute to different layers of mental accounts. For instance, an individual with both low and high aspiration levels can allocate part of his/her wealth to a lower layer (the safety-first principle) consisting of the fear of poverty or the goal of avoiding poverty and the other part of his/her wealth (high aspiration) to a higher layer that includes the potential to become rich. As explained by Shefrin and Statman (2000), the low and high aspiration levels lead to two different risky asset choices. Here, the first will prefer an asset closer to a risk-free asset and the latter will prefer something more like a "lottery ticket."

Using BPT, Shefrin and Statman (2000) were able to explain why individuals might buy bonds and lottery tickets at the same time. In other words, they clarified why individuals might be simultaneously risk averse and risk seeking and construct portfolios consisting of various combinations of these types of assets. They also investigated the implications of BPT for portfolio construction and security design.

5. Individual Portfolio Choice Behavior: An Experimental Research

The mean–variance (M–V) framework proposed by Markowitz (1952) is structured based on the rationality of individuals and the utility maximization principle, and it involves several assumptions that remain highly debated. For example, Roy (1952) focused on the definition of risk and criticized the use of standard deviation as a measure of risk. From the behavioral perspective, according to Weber et al. (2013) and Merkle (2018), there exists volatility neglect in observed investment decisions (Huber et al. 2019). Another criticism of M–V is related to the correlation coefficient, which is a linear dependence measure with an inability to model the co-movements at the tails of return distributions, in addition to not being invariant under strictly increasing non-linear transformations (Embrechts, et al. 2002). Returning to the behavioral perspective, it has also been shown that individuals ignore information about the correlation coefficient and/or covariance between the investment alternatives associated with an investment decision (Hedesstrom et al. 2006; Gubaydullina & Spiwoks, 2015; Cornil et. al., 2019). Moreover, several studies have shown that individuals prefer positive skewness and pay explicit attention to the probability of loss (Zeisberger, 2022).

Motivated by these research findings, this section aims to obtain the portfolio allocations of individuals and compare those allocations with the predictions of the traditional M–V portfolio. Additionally, researchers have recently been eager to utilize technological developments and employ various machine and deep learning algorithms to model and predict financial data. Following this stream of research, the second aim of this section is to predict the portfolio allocations of individuals by employing a deep neural network (DNN) algorithm with the weights initialized by a deep belief network (DBN), which is termed DBN-DNN.

To accomplish these aims, laboratory experiments were designed and conducted between November and December 2023 at the School of Business, Istanbul University.[1] The returns of two risky assets were simulated from the *t* copula with the marginals from a GARCH(1,1) process. First, the question of which portfolio allocation strategy would be able to capture and predict an individual portfolio choice closer to the experimental outcomes (actual allocations) will be assessed. Next, the applicability of a deep learning algorithm in terms of forecasting portfolio choice will be evaluated using the experimental outcomes and the DBN-DNN algorithm.

The remainder of this section briefly describes the theoretical background of the employed methodology, explains the experimental design, and reports the empirical findings of the analysis conducted on the experimental outcomes.

5.1. Theoretical Backgrounds

5.1.1. Copula Functions

Copulas are multivariate functions "linking" the univariate margins of a multivariate distribution (Sklar (1959). More formally, a joint multivariate distribution *F* can be defined in terms of the copula function *C* and *n* number of univariate marginals as follows:

$$F(x_1,\ldots,x_n) = C(F_1(x_1),\ldots,F_n(x_n)) \tag{5}$$

The variables of the margins are assumed to be both independent and identically distributed (i.i.d.). The copula function *C* modeling the dependence between the variables can be defined as follows:

$$C(u_1,\ldots,u_n;\theta) = F(F_1^{-1}(u_1),\ldots,F_n^{-1}(u_n)) \tag{6}$$

In Equation 6, the term θ represents the copula parameter, while $F_1^{-1},\ldots.,F_n^{-1}$ are the quantile functions with $F_i^{-1}(u) = inf\{x: F_i(x) \geq u\}$. As the asset returns are simulated from the *t* copula in this research, the

[1] The authors would like to thank Stefan Palan for his feedback on the experimental design of this research during the Experimental Finance 2023 Conference in Sofia as well as to Sascha Füllbrunn who critically assessed the experimental design and provided us with his feedback.

definition of a *two*-dimensional *t* copula (C_t) is given as follows (Demarta & McNeil, 2005):

$$C_t = \int_{-\infty}^{t_v^{-1}(u_1)} \int_{-\infty}^{t_v^{-1}(u_2)} \frac{\Gamma\left(\frac{v+2}{2}\right)}{\Gamma\left(\frac{v}{2}\right)\sqrt{(v\pi)^2|\boldsymbol{R}|}} \left(1 + \frac{\boldsymbol{X}^T\boldsymbol{R}^{-1}\boldsymbol{X}}{v}\right)^{-\frac{v+2}{2}} d\boldsymbol{X} \tag{7}$$

In Equation 7, v, $\boldsymbol{R}$, and t_v^{-1} represent the degrees of freedom parameter, correlation matrix, and inverse cdf of Student's t distribution, respectively.

5.1.2. DBN-DNN

A DNN is principally an artificial neural network (ANN) consisting of a deeper network structure with several layers and hidden units. A feed-forward ANN with randomly initialized weights is defined as follows:

$$y_k = f\left(\sum_{j=1}^{m}\left(x_j * \omega_{jk}\right) - \vartheta_k\right) \tag{8}$$

where y_k and x_j are the outputs of the hidden and input layers. $f(\cdot)$ is the activation function (a sigmoid in this case) and ϑ_k is the bias term. Moreover, the feed-forward output value (o_ℓ) of the output layer is:

$$o_\ell = f\left(\sum_{k=1}^{n}(y_k * \omega_{k\ell}) - \vartheta_\ell\right) \tag{9}$$

Instead of random weights, if a DNN uses the updated weights of a DBN as its initial weights, then the network is called a DBN-DNN (Deng, 2014). Proposed by Hinton et al. (2006), a DBN is a "Bayesian probabilistic generative model" with layers of simple models—namely, restricted Boltzmann machines (RBMs). An RBM is a type of Boltzmann machine with no connections between the hidden units and within the same layer. A DBN is constructed by *stacking* several layers of RBM (Deng, 2014).

In this section, the one-period-ahead average portfolio allocations of participants are predicted using several features as inputs for the DBN-DNN algorithm, which can be defined as follows:

$$w_{i,p}^* = f\left(r_{1,p-1}, \dots, r_{1,p-10}, r_{2,p-1}, \dots, r_{2,p-10}, \sigma_1, \sigma_2, \rho_{1,2}\right) + \varepsilon_p \tag{10}$$

where $w_{i,p}^*$ is the predicted investment weight of asset i ($i \in \{1,2,3\}$) for the period p. $r_{1,p-1}$ and $r_{2,p-1}$ are the actual returns of Asset 1 and Asset 2 observed by participants in period *p-1*, respectively. Moreover, σ_1 and σ_2 are the realized standard deviations of the returns of Asset 1 and Asset 2 observed until period p (consisting of all previous observations). $\rho_{1,2}$ represents the realized correlation between the two risky assets observed until period p, and ε_p is the error term.

5.1.3. Portfolio Allocation

An optimal portfolio in Markowitz's (1952) M–V framework occurs when there is a risk-free asset (referred to as a tangency or maximum Sharpe portfolio) (Sharpe, 1964; 1966):

$$M\!-V^* = max\left(\mu^T \omega - r_f\right) / \sqrt{\omega^T \Sigma \omega} \tag{11}$$

where μ and ω represent the mean and weight vector of the asset returns, respectively. The term r_f is the risk-free rate and Σ is the covariance matrix of the asset returns.

An equally weighted portfolio (EWP) simply assigns equal weights to each asset. For instance, if there are three assets (two risky assets and one risk-free asset), the portfolio weight of each asset will be as follows:

$$w_i = 1/3 \tag{12}$$

where w_i is the weight of asset *i* ($i \in \{1,2,3\}$).

5.1.4. Evaluation

The portfolio allocation prediction performance of the strategies is compared using the Euclidean distance, which is defined as follows (Rieskamp et al. 2003; Olschewski et al. 2021):

$$ED = \sum_{p=1}^{n} \sqrt{\sum_{i=1}^{3} \left(w_{i,p}^* - w_{i,p}\right)^2} \tag{13}$$

In Equation 13, $w_{i,p}$ is the asset *i* investment proportion in period p and $w_{i,p}^*$ is the portfolio allocation strategy-specific investment proportion (weight) in asset *i* for the period p.

5.2. The Experiment

We conducted laboratory experiments to test whether individual portfolio allocation decisions could be defined and/or predicted well by the chosen portfolio allocation strategies. For this purpose, we asked participants to make investment decisions involving three different financial assets (two risky and one safe) by allocating a certain endowment. The returns of the two risky assets were simulated from the *t* copula function with four degrees of freedom ($\nu = 4$) and with a rho that was equal to either $\rho = 0.75$ or $\rho = -0.75$. Additionally, the univariate marginals were simulated from the GARCH(1,1)–Student's t processes. While participants were informed about the main asset-specific statistics (e.g., mean return, standard deviation, correlation coefficient), the dependence structure between the risky assets and the distributional properties was not told and/or explained to them in advance of making their investment decisions.

5.2.1. Design

The design of our experiment consisted of two main treatments. While Treatment 1 was the high positive correlation group, Treatment 2 was the opposite. At the beginning of each session, which consisted of both treatments, the instructions were read aloud and presented on the computer screen and/or supplied as a printout so that participants could follow and independently re-read them. Prior to making their investment decisions, the main concepts (e.g., return, standard deviation, correlation coefficient) were thoroughly explained to the participants. Their understanding of these concepts was controlled with several follow-up questions.

The main investment decision part of the experiment began with a practice session in which participants tried and became familiar with the software by making ten investment decisions. Then, we asked participants to make their actual investment decisions involving the three assets by considering the information supplied with the instructions. The asset-specific investment amounts were restricted to between a minimum of zero and a maximum of their budget. Participants were expected to allocate all their budget in each investment decision. Moreover, borrowing and/or short selling was not allowed. The descriptive statistics of the actual returns of the two risky assets simulated from the *t* copula with GARCH(1,1) marginals and used in the main part of the experiment (the actual 30 investment decisions) are summarized in Table 1.

Table 1. Descriptive Statistics of the Two Risky Assets

Treatment	Asset	Mean	Median	Standard Deviation	Minimum	Maximum
1	Asset 1	0.0241	0.0257	0.0213	-0.0120	0.0786
	Asset 2	0.0443	0.0422	0.0545	-0.0478	0.1744
2	Asset 1	0.0241	0.0270	0.0227	-0.0578	0.0590
	Asset 2	0.0415	0.0410	0.0563	-0.0514	0.2449

Following the main investment part, Holt and Laury's (2002) lottery choice task and a demographic questionnaire were completed by participants to conclude the experiment. The practice session and the main investment decision part of the experiment, including the risk attitude elicitation task and the final demographic questionnaire, were computerized using z-Tree (Fischbacher, 2007). A sample of the decision screen of the experiment is shown in Figure 1.

5.2.2. Participants

Five sessions of the experiment were conducted on November 6 and 7, 2023 at the School of Business, Istanbul University. The remaining nine sessions were conducted on December 18, 19, and 20, 2023. The duration of each session was approximately 45 minutes. Participants were recruited from among the students attending Istanbul University's School of Business and randomly assigned to the sessions and two treatments.

Overall, a total of 125 students participated in the experiment. However, we limited the sample size of this research to 56 students who made consistent decisions during Holt and Laury's (2002) risk attitude elicitation task and whose answers were found to be satisfactory during the follow-up questions.

Among the 56 participants, 28 faced the high positive correlation treatment (Treatment 1) and 28 faced the high negative correlation treatment (Treatment 2). The mean age of the participants was 24 years (range: 19–43 years). The participants' demographics are summarized in Table 2.

Your budget: 995.04

Asset 1 investment amount:

Asset 2 investment amount:

Remainder: Your total investment amount cannot exceed your budget

Continue

Investment Decision	Asset 1 (% return)	Asset 1 investment amount (TL)	Asset 1 earnings (TL)	Asset 2 (% return)	Asset 2 investment amount (TL)	Asset 2 Earning (TL)	Asset 3 (% return)	Asset 3 investment amount (TL)	Asset 3 earnings (TL)	Portfolio Return (%)	Portfolio Value (TL)
1	5.00	100.00	5.00	-4.00	200.00	-8.00	1.00	700.00	7.00	0.40	1004
2	-2.00	500.00	-10.00	-1.00	200.00	-2.00	1.00	304.00	3.04	-0.89	995.04

Source: Authors' own illustration.

Figure 1. English Translation of the Investment Decision Screen.

Table 2. Demographics of Participants

Treatment	Sample Size (n)	Mean Age	Male/ Female	Single/ Married	Education (cont.)	Subject of Education	Finance Lecture/ Education
Treatment 1	28	24.5	19/9	26/2	Undergraduate: 19; Masters: 9	Business/Economics etc.: 28	Yes: 11/No: 17
Treatment 2	28	23.4	20/8	28/0	Undergraduate: 22; Masters: 6	Business/Economics etc.: 27; Other Social Sciences: 1	Yes: 14/ No: 14

5.3. Empirical Findings

After the participant data were obtained, the z-Tree files were transferred to R software (R Core Team, 2023) and the rest of the data analyses were conducted in R v4.3.1 (R Core Team, 2023). The period- and treatment-specific mean values of the portfolio weights of the three assets are shown in Figures 2 and 3, respectively.

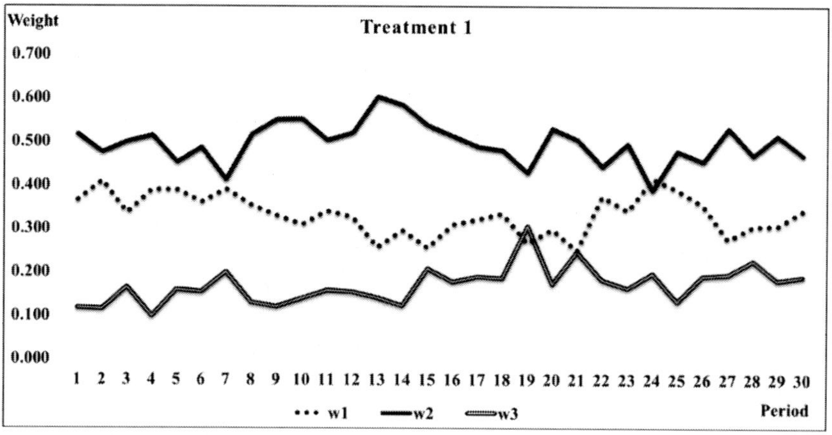

Source: Authors' own illustration.

Figure 2. Average Portfolio Weights – Treatment 1.

As can be seen from Figures 2 and 3, while the average w_2 (the proportion of the budget invested in Asset 2 averaged across the participants in each treatment) was mainly higher in both treatments (Treatment 1 w_2: mean = 0.5 (0.28)[1]; Treatment 2 w_2: mean = 0.51 (0.3)), on average, the high positive correlation group invested a larger amount of their budget in Asset 3 (Treatment 1 w_3: mean = 0.17 (0.25); Treatment 2 w_3: mean = 0.13 (0.19)), with an increasing proportion of safe asset investment over the studied periods. The divergence between the weights of the risky assets and the substitution between the weights of risky Asset 1 and the safe asset over the different periods in the positive correlation group can also be observed in Figure 2.

Moreover, the average investment proportion in terms of Asset 1 was higher in Treatment 2 than in Treatment 1 (Treatment 1 w_1: mean = 0.33 (0.24); Treatment 2 w_1: mean = 0.36 (0.30)). Nevertheless, according to the applied *t*-test and the non-parametric Mann–Whitney U test, the treatment-

[1] Standard deviation in parenthesis.

specific average investment proportions in relation to the assets were not significantly different (*t*-test: w_1 (*p=0.58*), w_2 (*p=0.77*), w_3 (*p=0.35*); Mann-Whitney U: w_1 (*U=358, p=0.58*), w_2 (*U=366, p=0.68*), w_3 (*U=457, p=0.29*)).

Furthermore, the participants in Treatment 1 and Treatment 2 were, on average, risk averse and made 4.64 (2.31) and 4.71 (2.14) safe choices during the Holt and Laury's (2002) lottery choice task, respectively. The applied *t*-test ($p = 0.91$) and Mann–Whitney U test ($U = 367, p = 0.68$) confirmed the statistically insignificant difference between the number of safe choices for the treatments. The treatment differences between the participant-specific properties (e.g., age, gender, etc.) were also assessed using the *t*-test and Mann–Whitney U test. Table 3 reports the relevant statistics and the corresponding *p*-values.

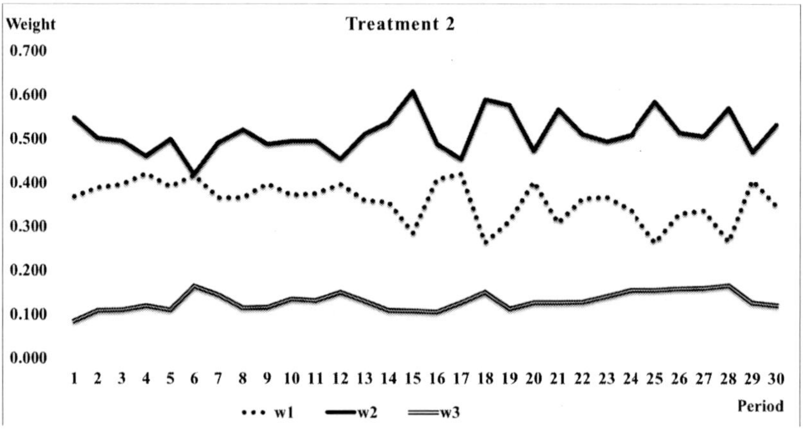

Source: Authors' own illustration.

Figure 3. Average Portfolio Weights – Treatment 2.

Table 3. Treatment Differences in Participants

Property	t-test (p-value)	Mann-Whitney U (p-value)
Age	0.86 (0.39)	355.5 (0.55)
Gender	0.29 (0.78)	406 (1)
Education	0.89 (0.37)	434 (0.55)
Finance Education	-0.8 (0.43)	350 (0.59)

According to the applied Spearman correlation, there was a significant negative correlation between the participants' age and the Asset 2 average investment (w_2) in Treatment 1 ($\rho = -0.35, p = 0.035$), as well as a significant positive correlation between the participants' age and the w_3 in both treatments (Treatment 1: $\rho = 0.26, p = 0.09$ (at 10% significance level); Treatment 2: $\rho = 0.35, p = 0.032$). In Treatment 2, the correlation between the participants' age and the w_1 was also significant at a 10% significance level ($\rho = -0.31, p = 0.055$).

When the gender of the participants was considered, there was a significant negative Spearman correlation between the average Asset 3 investment proportion and the gender in Treatment 1 ($\rho = -0.49, p = 0.004$). On average, women invested lesser amounts of their budget in Asset 3 in Treatment 1. By contrast, there was a significant negative correlation between the w_2 and financial education ($\rho = -0.493, p = 0.0038$) in Treatment 1. Participants who indicated that they had education/training in finance and/or investment management invested, on average, a lesser proportion of their budget in Asset 2 when compared with participants who did not report having financial education in Treatment 1. Moreover, the participants with financial education invested a significantly larger proportion of their budget in Asset 3 in Treatment 1 ($\rho = 0.37, p = 0.028$) when compared with the w_3 of the participants without financial education. In Treatment 2, none of the estimated Spearman correlations between the participants' average investment proportions in one of the assets and their financial education were significant.

In addition, in Treatment 1, there was a significant negative and a significant positive Spearman correlation between the average w_2 ($\rho = -0.54, p = 0.002$) and the average w_3 ($\rho = 0.40, p = 0.017$) of participants and their education level. Participants studying for a master's degree invested a significantly smaller proportion of their budget in Asset 2 and a significantly larger proportion in Asset 3 when compared with the participants studying on an undergraduate program. However, the estimated correlations were not significant in Treatment 2.

Table 4. Euclidean Distance (ED) Estimates of the Methods

Method 1	Treatment 1	Treatment 2
EWP	4.563	5.623
M–V*	12.172	9.316
DBN-DNN	1.643	1.262

[1] The Euclidean distance of each method estimated for the last 20 periods (investment decisions).

Finally, with regard to the evaluation of the portfolio allocation strategies, Table 4 reports the estimated accuracy metrics, showing the ability of the applied strategies to predict an individual portfolio choice in terms of their divergence (distance) from the observed participant data.

The treatment- and strategy-specific EDs were estimated for each period from the average of the participants' investment proportions and then their sum was obtained. According to Table 4, the one-period-ahead weight forecasts of the DBN-DNN obtained the smallest EDs, indicating the better individual portfolio choice prediction ability of the algorithm when compared with the other methods applied in this research. The participants' portfolio allocations were not close to the fit and the predictions of the tangency portfolio (M–V*). However, based on the three allocation strategies that did not employ observed past allocation data (since the average portfolio allocations of the participants in the first ten periods were used to train the DBN-DNN), the EWP obtained the smallest EDs from the actual observations.

Conclusion

The first section of this chapter reviewed the definition and behavioral characteristics of *economic man*. Then, it reported some well-known violations concerning the *homo economicus* model, such as the Allais paradox, violations of the axioms of rational choice, as well as heuristics and biases. The following three sections (sections two to four) discussed the cornerstones of the behavioral aspects of portfolio choice under risk and uncertainty. These sections briefly explained the theories integrating behavioral insights into the portfolio choice problem and were able to significantly differentiate them from the traditional M–V framework, such as the PT of Kahneman and Tversky (1979), the SP/A theory of Lopes (1987), and the BPT of Shefrin and Statman (2000).

In the final section of this chapter, individual portfolio choice behavior was assessed by employing experiments in a controlled laboratory setting. The participants were recruited from among the students at the School of Business of Istanbul University, with announcements concerning the research made during lectures and sent by email. They were asked to invest a certain amount of an endowment (budget) among three assets (two risky and a risk-free asset) repeatedly during 30 periods. The returns of the two assets (Asset 1 and Asset 2) were simulated from the *t* copula. As a result, they had a dependence structure defined by the specified copula type and its parameters. The obtained participant dataset was analyzed and compared with two of the commonly employed portfolio allocation strategies found in the literature—namely, the

EWP and the tangency portfolio—using a 1% risk-free asset. In addition to these portfolio allocation strategies, a deep learning algorithm (DBN-DNN) was applied to predict the one-period-ahead treatment and period-specific average portfolio weights of the participants.

The portfolio allocations of the strategies were compared with a distance measure known as the ED, which has been employed in several prior studies, such as Rieskamp et al. (2003), Olschewski et al. (2021), and de Castro et al. (2022). According to the estimated strategy- and treatment-specific values of the measure, DBN-DNN yielded the best values in both treatments, indicating the applicability of the algorithm in individual portfolio allocation prediction tasks. The EWP obtained the second-best ED values, whereas the M–V* is ranked as the worst approach. Nevertheless, it is important to note that this chapter employed the past portfolio allocations of the participants to train the DBN-DNN algorithm (see the DBN-DNN section for all the features), which might not be available to a researcher or an analyst trying to predict individual portfolio allocation with market data. In such a case, an unsupervised algorithm will likely be more suitable for similar tasks.

References

Allais, M. (1953). Le Comportement de l'Homme Rationnel Devant Le Risque: Critique Des Postulats et Axiomes de l'Ecole Americaine [The Behavior of the Rational Man under Risk: Criticism of the Postulates and Axioms of the American School]. *Econometrica*, *21*(4), 503–546. https://doi.org/10.2307/1907921.

Barnes, T. J. (1988). Rationality and Relativism in Economic Geography: An Interpretive Review of the Homo Economicus Assumption. *Progress in Human Geography*, *12*(4), 473–496.

Chen, J. M. (2016). *Finance and the Behavioral Prospect: Risk, Exuberance, and Abnormal Markets*. Palgrave Macmillan Cham. https://doi.org/10.1007/978-3-319-32711-2.

Cornil, Y., Hardisty, D. J., & Bart, Y. (2019). Easy, Breezy, Risky: Lay Investors Fail to Diversify Because Correlated Assets Feel More Fluent and Less Risky. *Organizational Behavior and Human Decision Processes*, *153*, 103–117.

de Castro, L., Galvao, A. F., Kim, J. Y., Montes-Rojas, G., & Olmo, J. (2022). Experiments on Portfolio Selection: A Comparison between Quantile Preferences and Expected Utility Decision Models. *Journal of Behavioral and Experimental Economics*, *97*, 101822. https://doi.org/10.1016/j.socec.2021.101822.

Demarta, S., & McNeil, A. J. (2005). The t Copula and Related Copulas. *International Statistical Review*, *73*(1), 111–129. https://doi.org/10.1111/j.1751-5823.2005.tb00254.x.

Deng, L. (2014). A Tutorial Survey of Architectures, Algorithms, and Applications for Deep Learning. *APSIPA Transactions on Signal and Information Processing*, *3*(1), 1–29. https://doi.org/10.1017/atsip.2013.9.

Embrechts, P., McNeil, A., & Straumann, D. (2002). Correlation and Dependence in Risk Management: Properties and Pitfalls. In M. A. H. Dempster (Ed.) *Risk Management: Value at Risk and Beyond* (pp. 176–223). Cambridge University Press.

Fischbacher, U. (2007). Z-tree: Zurich Toolbox for Ready-Made Economic Experiments. *Experimental Economics*, *10*(2), 171–178.

Gigerenzer, G., & Gaissmaier, W. (2011). Heuristic Decision Making. *Annual Review of Psychology*, *62*, 451–482.

Gubaydullina, Z., & Spiwoks, M. (2015). Correlation Neglect, Naïve Diversification, and Irrelevant Information as Stumbling Blocks for Optimal Diversification. *Journal of Finance and Investment Analysis*, *4*(2), 1–19.

Hinton, G. E., Osindero, S., & Teh, Y. (2006). A Fast Learning Algorithm for Deep Belief Nets. *Neural Computation*, *18*(7), 1527–1554. https://doi.org/10.1162/neco.2006.18.7.1527.

Hedesstrom, T. M., Svedsater, H., & Garling, T. (2006). Covariation Neglect among Novice Investors. *Journal of Experimental Psychology-Applied*, *12*(3), 155–165. https://doi.org/10.1037/1076-898x.12.3.155.

Holt, C. A., & Laury, S. K. (2002). Risk Aversion and Incentive Effects, *American Economic Review*, *92*(5), 1644–1655.

Huber, J., Palan, S., & Zeisberger, S. (2019). Does Investor Risk Perception Drive Asset Prices in Markets? Experimental Evidence. *Journal of Banking and Finance*, 105635. https://doi.org/10.1016/j.jbankfin.2019.105635.

Kahneman, D., & Tversky, A. (1979). Prospect Theory: An Analysis of Decision under Risk. *Econometrica*, *47*(2), 263–292.

Lopes, L. L. (1987). Between Hope and Fear: The Psychology of Risk. *Advances in Experimental Social Psychology*, *20*, 255–295. https://doi.org/10.1016/S0065-2601(08)60416-5.

Markowitz, H. (1952). Portfolio Selection*. *The Journal of Finance*, *7*(1), 77–91.

Merkle, C. (2018). The Curious Case of Negative Volatility. *Journal of Financial Markets*, *40*, 92–108. https://doi.org/10.1016/j.finmar.2017.11.001.

Mill, J. S. (1836). On the Definition of Political Economy; and on the Method of Investigation Proper to It. *London and Westminster Review*, *26*(1), 1–29.

Mischel, W. (1968). *Personality and Assessment*. John Wiley & Sons, Ltd.

Olschewski, S., Diao, L., & Rieskamp, J. (2021). Reinforcement Learning about Asset Variability and Correlation in Repeated Portfolio Decisions. *Journal of Behavioral and Experimental Finance*, *32*, 100559. https://doi.org/10.1016/j.jbef.2021.100559.

R Core Team (2023). R: A Language and Environment for Statistical Computing. R Foundation for Statistical Computing, Vienna, Austria. https://www.R-project.org/.

Rengifo, E. W., Trendafilov, R., & Trifan, E. (2014). Behavioral Portfolio Theory and Investment Management. In H. K. Baker (Ed.) *Investor Behavior: The Psychology of Financial Planning and Investing* (pp. 421–438). John Wiley & Sons, Ltd.

Rieskamp, J., Busemeyer, J. R., & Laine, T. (2003). How Do People Learn to Allocate Resources? Comparing Two Learning Theories. *Journal of Experimental Psychology:*

Learning, Memory, and Cognition, *29*(6), 1066–1081. https://doi.org/10.1037/0278-7393.29.6.1066.
Roy, A. D. (1952). Safety-First and the Holding of Assets. *Econometrica*, *20*(3), 431–449.
Sharpe, W. F. (1964). Capital Asset Prices: A Theory of Market Equilibrium Under Conditions of Risk*. *The Journal of Finance*, *19*(3), 425–442. https://doi.org/10.1111/j.1540-6261.1964.tb02865.x.
Sharpe, W. F. (1966). Mutual Fund Performance. *The Journal of Business*, *39*(1), 119–138.
Shefrin, H., & Statman, M. (2000). Behavioral Portfolio Theory. *The Journal of Financial and Quantitative Analysis*, *35*(2), 127–151.
Simon, H. A. (1955). A Behavioral Model of Rational Choice. *Quarterly Journal of Economics, 69*, 99–118.
Sklar, A. (1959). Fonctions de répartition à n dimensions et leurs marges [N-dimensional distribution functions and their margins]. *Annales de l'ISUP*, *8*(3), 229–231.
Tversky, A. (1975). A Critique of Expected Utility Theory: Descriptive and Normative Considerations. *Erkenntnis*, *9*, 163–173.
Tversky, A., & Kahneman, D. (1992). Advances in Prospect Theory: Cumulative Representation of Uncertainty. *Journal of Risk and Uncertainty*, *5*, 297–323.
Urbina, D. A., & Ruiz-Villaverde, A. (2019). A Critical Review of Homo Economicus from Five Approaches. *American Journal of Economics and Sociology*, *78*(1), 63–93. https://doi.org/10.1111/ajes.12258.
von Neumann, J., & Morgenstern, O. (1944). *The Theory of Games and Economic Behavior* (2nd ed.). Princeton University Press.
Weber, M., Weber, E. U., & Nosić, A. (2013). Who takes Risks When and Why: Determinants of Changes in Investor Risk Taking*. *Review of Finance*, *17*(3), 847–883. https://doi.org/10.1093/rof/rfs024.
Wilkinson, N., & Klaes, M. (2012). *An Introduction to Behavioral Economics* (2nd ed.). Palgrave Macmillan.
Zeisberger, S. (2022). Do People Care about Loss Probabilities? *Journal of Risk and Uncertainty*, *65*, 185–213. https://doi.org/10.1007/s11166-022-09391-y.

Chapter 4

Rank Statistics and Asset Allocation

Cemile Özgür[1,*], PhD
and Vedat Sarikovanlik[2], PhD
[1]Department of Management Information Systems, Boğaziçi University, Istanbul, Türkiye
[2]Department of Finance, Istanbul University, Istanbul, Türkiye

Abstract

This chapter begins by providing a brief introduction to several terms and concepts that are used throughout the text, such as ranks, rank statistics, and bibliometrics. The second section presents the methodology and results of a bibliometric analysis of the literature concerning the applications of ranks and/or rank statistics in the portfolio allocation context. While there is an increasing trend toward conducting bibliometric analysis, to the best of our knowledge, this is the first bibliometric analysis of the literature employing ranks and/or ranks statistics in asset allocation. Furthermore, section three applies a recently proposed rank-based asset allocation strategy to an exchange-traded fund portfolio and compares its results to those of several other portfolio allocation methods—namely, the global minimum variance, Min-CVaR, tangency, and maximum diversification portfolios. The last section discusses the research methodologies applied in the second and third sections, the results obtained in each section, as well as their limitations.

Keywords: rank, rank statistics, portfolio allocation, bibliometric analysis, rank-based approach

---

* Corresponding Author's Email: cemile.ozgur@pt.bogazici.edu.tr / ozgurcemile@yahoo.com

In: Asset Allocation: Theory, Recent Developments and Beyond
Editors: Cemile Özgür and Vedat Sarikovanlik
ISBN: 979-8-89530-649-9

1. Rank Statistics

The term *rank* refers to the particular position of someone or something in relation to others. Since statistics is the science of revealing information based on numerical facts and measurements, the term *rank statistics* refers to any type of function involving ranks that define the numerical position of a variable in relation to others, following an ordering practice of the variables. In this sense, the ranking of the variables is performed with reference to the orders or *order statistics* of the variables. As a result, rank statistics are also referred to as *rank order statistics* (Sen, 2006).

While the roots of order statistics can be traced back to Ptolemy (circa 150 AD), it was Wilks who introduced the term in 1942 (David, 2006). The terms order statistics (OS) and rank statistics (RS) are sometimes used interchangeably, although they are not the same. While OS deal with the practices of ordering random variables, their properties, and the associated functions (David & Nagaraja, 2006), RS are typically defined as either linear or non-linear functions of ranks (Sen, 2006; Taniguchi et al. 2018).

More formally, let us assume that we have an independent random sample of $X = \{x_j\}_{j=1}^{l}$ for $j = 1, \ldots, l$. Let $\boldsymbol{R_j} = (R_1, \ldots, R_l)$ be the vector of ranks of x_j obtained by sorting the random variables in ascending order, which can be shown as follows:

$$x_{(1)} \leq x_{(2)} \leq \cdots \leq x_{(l)} \quad (1)$$

The random vector of $\boldsymbol{X}_{(r)} = (x_{(1)}, \ldots x_{(l)})$ including the ordered values in Equation 1 is defined as the OS of the sample X $(r = 1, \ldots, l)$. In other words, $x_{(r)}$ the rth value of the ordered sample in Equation 1 is termed the *rth order statistic*.

Moreover, the rank R_j shows the position number of x_j in the OS. For instance, the OS of the random sample of $X = \{10, 1, 5\}$ are $x_{(1)} = 1$, $x_{(2)} = 5$, and $x_{(3)} = 10$. The ranks of the variables of X are $R_1 = 3$, $R_2 = 1$, and $R_3 = 2$. As a result, Equation 2 holds true if the variables have a unique value. In other words, if the variables are different from each other and there are no ties.

$$x_j = x_{(R_j)} \quad (2)$$

In the case of ties, the averages of all r indices yielding $x_j = x_{(r)}$ are estimated. For instance, the rank of each variable of $X = \{10, 5, 1, 5\}$ is $R_1 = 4$, $R_2 = 2.5$, $R_3 = 1$, and $R_4 = 2.5$.

Furthermore, any type of function of ranks, such as $\mathcal{F}(R_j)$, is defined as an RS. Examples of well-known RS include Wilcoxon's (1945) rank sum and the signed rank tests, as well as the rank test statistics for independence, such as Spearman's rank correlation coefficient and Kendall's tau (Kendall, 1962). More recently, Kwon and Satchell (2024) introduced a new concept in RS known as *co-quantiles*. According to researchers, co-quantiles generalize OS, quantiles, and *concomitants* by enabling the recording and ranking of different attributes of a population among varying time periods. Concomitants are obtained by sorting a random sample depending on the corresponding values of a different sample. Ordering sample data and employing RS for various tasks represent common applications in statistics, economics, and finance. The main reason is that when compared with parametric methods, RS, as non-parametric methods based on ranks, are also applicable to ordinal data, giving the possibility of obtaining more robust estimations. As discussed by Sen (2006), the use of non-parametric methods based on ranks or signed ranks is not a new phenomenon in the statistics literature. RS have a fundamental role in a wide range of problems, including a genuine interest in practice.

2. Applications of Ranks in Portfolio Allocation: A Bibliometric Analysis

This section presents the methodology and results of a bibliometric analysis of the literature related to the applications of ranks and/or RS in the portfolio allocation context. First, we introduce and explain the basics of *bibliometric analysis* so that the reader has a better understanding of the methodology. Then, we provide explanations of the research methodology applied and the results obtained.

2.1. Bibliometrics

The term *bibliometrics* refers to the use of quantitative methods (e.g., mathematics and statistics) to analyze the bibliographic features or data of a certain body of literature (Lawani, 1981). According to Osareh (1996), while it was Pritchard (1969) who first coined the term bibliometrics, its usage actually dates back to the 1890s. Historically, the work by Campbell (1896) is considered to be one of the earliest attempts at bibliometric research (Sengupta, 1992). Moreover, E. Wyndham Hulme employed the term statistical bibliography in 1923. After that, the term *statistical bibliography* was periodically used until it was found to be unsatisfactory and replaced by the term bibliometrics in 1969. Conversely, while Ranganathan proposed the term *librametry* in 1948, Nalimov and Mulchenko (1969) employed the term *scientometrics* (Sengupta, 1992; Osareh, 1996).

Pritchard (1969:349) defined bibliometrics as "the application of mathematics and statistical methods to books and other media of communication." According to the Oxford English Dictionary, it is "the branch of library science" that employs mathematical and statistical tools to analyze a bibliography, such as articles, books, or other scientific publications. Osareh (1996) argued that the aim of bibliometrics is to enhance the development of scientific documentation, communication, and information processes by quantitatively analyzing literature and library services. The reader can consult the works by Osareh (1996), Hood and Wilson (2001), and Salini (2016) for a more detailed discussion on the definitions of various terms that could potentially be confused with bibliometrics, such as librametry, scientometrics, informetrics, and cybermetrics.

While bibliometrics is a recently developed field of science, there is an increasing trend of conducting bibliometric analysis (BA) of academic research due to technological developments and the increasing number of journals and scientific publications. In fact, BA is currently regarded as a highly significant tool for the assessment of academic outputs (Costa et al. 2019). There are also several journals that focus on discussions and issues concerning bibliometrics, such as *the Journal of Informetrics*, *Scientometrics*, and *Journal of Scientometric Research*.

2.2. Research Methodology

As the first step in a BA is clearly defined as the identification of applications of ranks and/or RS in the portfolio allocation context, the following subsections delve deeper into the other stages of the research, including the definition of the search procedures (keywords, database, search filters, etc.) and the software employed to collect, structure, and conduct a BA of the literature related to the chosen object of analysis.

Moreover, we aim to answer the following three research questions after analyzing the bibliographic data:

- R1: How many documents are already published on the related literature? How has the number of publications evolved over time?
- R2: What are the prominent studies, authors, and affiliations on the related literature?
- R3: What is the conceptual structure of the identified literature?

2.2.1. Search Tools: Database and Keywords

Among the three principal databases—*Web of Science* (WoS), *Scopus*, and *Google Scholar*—that are mainly used to extract publications for BA, this chapter employs WoS to search for publications related to the specified literature. Several research studies have conducted BA on data obtained from only the WoS database, such as Liu et al. (2014), Prado et al. (2016), Qasim (2017), Costa et al. (2017), Costa et al. (2019), Zhou et al. (2020), Secinaro et al. (2021), Qudah et al. (2024), and Bahoo et al. (2024).

Keyword selection is an important aspect of BA. This chapter employed the following independent keyword search combinations (Search 1, Search 2, etc.) in the WoS database, using the Boolean operator AND to extract related literature featuring all the specified search terms:

Search 1: Topic = "rank" AND "portfolio*"; Search 2: Topic = "rank" AND "robust portfolio*"; Search 3: Topic = "rank based approach"; Search 4: Topic = "rank based" AND "stock selection"; Search 5: Topic = "cross-sectional momentum*"; Search 6: Topic = "quantile portfolio*".

The following search specifications were applied to all six keyword searches (Search 1, Search 2, etc.):

Timespan = "all year"; Languages = "English"; Document Types = "Article" or "Early Access" or "Book Chapters" or "Review Article"; Databases: "Web of Science Core Collection".

The first keyword search (Search 1) yielded 717 results. After we limited the results to English-language documents of the types specified above, there were 617 documents left. Similarly, Search 2, Search 3, Search 4, Search 5, and Search 6 yielded 6, 73, 2, 33, and 6 documents, respectively, after filtering for the language and document type. Additionally, Search 5 and Search 6 consisted of the search terms "cross-sectional momentum*" and "quantile portfolio*". Cross-sectional momentum refers to the trading activities of investors wherein ranks of asset returns are used to construct investment portfolios by buying (selling) a certain number of the top (worst) performing assets based on their ranks. By contrast, quantile portfolios are constructed by first ordering the returns of assets and then dividing them into a specified number of quantiles. The assets belonging to a certain quantile are invested by equal weights or other varying proportions, depending on the investor's preferences. The reader can consult Özgür and Sarıkovanlık (2024) for a discussion on the different portfolio allocation strategies that use the univariate and/or cross-sectional ranks of asset returns. In any case, the first keyword search (Search 1) had already covered many of the documents listed in the rest of the searches.

In the next step, the title, abstract, and keywords of all the documents were reviewed to control the suitability of the literature's content. While there were many publications that used the words "rank" and "portfolio" in their title, abstract, or keywords, they mainly employed various methods of portfolio allocation without any application of ranks or RS-related methods in this context. Those publications that used only ranks to order the performance or other properties of the constructed portfolios were excluded from the analysis because they did not apply any type of rank or RS-related method in portfolio allocation tasks. However, in addition to the publications that directly employed rank-based methods/approaches in portfolio allocation, the ones that ranked the return/price forecasts of various methods or other properties of assets to construct a portfolio were included in the analysis. Overall, 83 publications (book chapters and both early access and review articles) that used ranks and/or RS in the portfolio construction/allocation context were identified and used in the next step of the bibliometric research.

2.2.2. The Software

The BibTeX file of the collected literature, including the full record and the references, was extracted from the WoS database and transferred to the R software (R Core Team, 2023). After the file was loaded into the R software, it was controlled and converted to a data frame with cases corresponding to the Field Tags of the WoS by using the *bibliometrix* (Aria & Cuccurullo, 2017) package in R. Then, the converted data frame was exported as an Excel (*.xlsx*) file by using the *xlsx* (Dragulescu & Arendt, 2020) package in R.

We employed the *biblioshiny* plug-in of the R software for the bibliographic data analysis and the visualization of the results. The reason for this is that biblioshiny is compatible with both text and BibTeX files and has various functionalities enabling high-quality visualization of the outputs of a bibliographic data analysis. These and several other properties of biblioshiny that ease the bibliographic data analysis process are discussed by Qudah et al. (2024) and Ge et al. (2022).

2.3. Research Results

This subsection presents the results of the BA of the carefully filtered and selected academic literature related to the use of ranks and/or RS in the portfolio allocation context in terms of various document attributes, including the authors, keywords, affiliations, and cited references.

2.3.1. Descriptive Analysis

The retrieved bibliographic data consisted of 83 documents published from 1993 to 2024. When the descriptive statistics of the data reported in Table 1 are analyzed, it can be seen that the documents included in the BA were published in 63 different sources, with an annual growth rate of 8.35%. This high annual publication growth rate highlights the recent interest of researchers, especially in the last five years, in the related literature and the literature's dynamic nature. Additionally, Figure 1 shows the development over time of the scientific outputs of the retrieved literature.

Table 1. Descriptives of the Data

Variable	Results	Variable	Results
Publication year (timespan)	1993:2024	Number of authors	190
Sources (journals, books, etc.)	63	Documents with single-authors	15
Documents	83	Co-authors per publication	2.48
Annual growth rate (%)	8.35	International co-authorships (%)	27.71
Document average age	7.43	Document types	
Average citations per document	65.95	Article	79
References	2468	Book chapter	1
Author's keywords	334	Article; early access	1
Keywords plus	201	Article; proceedings paper	2

According to Table 1, most of the collected documents were articles, with 65.95 citations on average. There were 190 researchers who contributed to the field, with 15 of them being the single author of a publication. Thus, approximately 82% of the documents had more than one author. The average number of authors per publication was 2.48. Among the 175 authors who collaborated with other researchers, 27.71% had international co-authors. Moreover, the documents had 2468 references, with 334 authors' keywords and 201 keywords plus that were included in the BA. The United States of America (USA), China, the United Kingdom (UK), Australia, and Canada were ranked as the top 5 countries out of 24, with a total of 23, 13, 7, 5, and 5 documents, respectively.

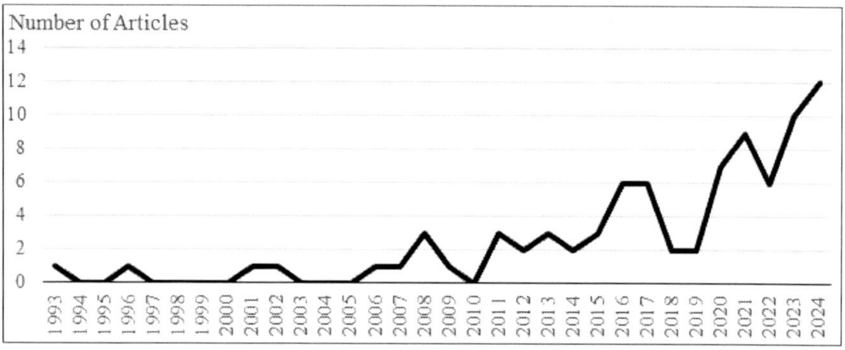

Source: Authors' own illustration.

Figure 1. Time Development of Annual Scientific Outputs.

Furthermore, Table 2 reports the top 30% of author affiliations (37 out of 124) ranked based on their scientific outputs (number of documents/articles), as well as alphabetically in the case of an equal number of articles. The top five most relevant sources ranked based on their total publication quantity in the specified research field were as follows: *North American Journal of Economics and Finance, Journal of Asset Management, Mathematical Finance, Quantitative Finance,* and *Annals of Finance*. Moreover, Oh Kang Kwon, Stephen Satchell, Zuo Quan Xu, Jiangfeng Li, and Ming Liu were ranked as the top five most productive authors based on their total number of contributions to the relevant literature. Among the 190 authors, Narasimhan Jegadeesh, Sheridan Titman, Oh Kang Kwon, Stephen Satchell, and Zuo Quan Xu were the top five most frequently cited authors. Furthermore, the top five most frequently cited documents were Jegadeesh and Titman (1993), Hartzmark (2015), Dorfleitner et al. (2020), Liu et al. (2011), and Song et al. (2017).

Table 2. Most Relevant Affiliations

Affiliation	Output	Affiliation	Output
UNIV SYDNEY	9	UNIV SOUTHAMPTON	3
HONG KONG POLYTECH UNIV	8	UNIV WATERLOO	3
COLUMBIA UNIV	6	UNIV WISCONSIN	3
RENMIN UNIV CHINA	6	UNIV WITWATERSRAND	3
UNIV CAMBRIDGE	6	XIAMEN UNIV	3
UNIV TORONTO	6	YORK UNIV	3
LAPPEENRANTA UNIV TECHNOL	5	AUSTRALIAN NATL UNIV	2
CHINESE UNIV HONG KONG	4	CHENGDU UNIV TECHNOL	2
EAST CHINA UNIV SCI AND TECHNOL	4	CHONGQING TECHNOL AND BUSINESS UNIV	2
IOWA STATE UNIV	4	CHRIST UNIV	2
JINAN UNIV	4	CLAREMONT MCKENNA COLL	2
MASSEY UNIV	4	CTR INVEST MATEMAT	2
EDHEC BUSINESS SCH	3	ERASMUS UNIV	2
GYEONGSANG NATL UNIV	3	FORDHAM UNIV	2
HUNAN UNIV	3	HEINRICH HEINE UNIV DUSSELDORF	2
NATL YANG MING CHIAO TUNG UNIV	3	HSE UNIV	2
UNIV MISSOURI	3	INT COLL	2
UNIV OXFORD	3	ISTANBUL UNIV	2
UNIV RICHMOND	3		

2.3.2. Conceptual Analysis

Based on the analysis performed to identify the conceptual structure of the retrieved data, Figure 2 shows the identified clusters by applying a multiple correspondence analysis (MCA) to the abstracts of the data. These three clusters indicate the common concepts in the documents using the top 60 words. The words with similar distributions are represented closer on the map.

According to Figure 2, the first and biggest cluster (shown by the connected solid lines) consisted of research using the terms cross-sectional, time series, momentum, strategies, returns, stock, markets, investors, and factors in the abstracts. The second biggest cluster (shown by the connected dashed lines) included papers employing the terms return, stocks, portfolio, selection, rank, based, portfolio, model(s), method, and investment in the abstracts. The third and the smallest cluster consisted of research using the terms asset(s), expected, risk, provide, empirical, and paper. As can be inferred from the terms commonly employed in the abstracts, the papers that used momentum strategies (cross-sectional and/or time series momentum) or various factors constituted the first cluster of literature. Examples of the papers in the first cluster include works by Jagedeesh and Titman (1993), Tse (2015), Liu et al. (2011), and Ham et al. (2019). Conversely, examples of the papers in the third cluster include works by Patari et al. (2012), Donaldson et al. (2011), Chen and Xiang (2016), and Xu (2016). Overall, the three clusters were able to differentiate and group the literature based on the applications of ranks and/or RS in the portfolio allocation context depending on the commonly employed terms or concepts leading to the identification and extraction of the cluster-specific research methodology and conceptual structure of the papers. This is not surprising, given that the purpose of an abstract is to communicate or explain the main objective, methodology, and results of a paper in a concise manner.

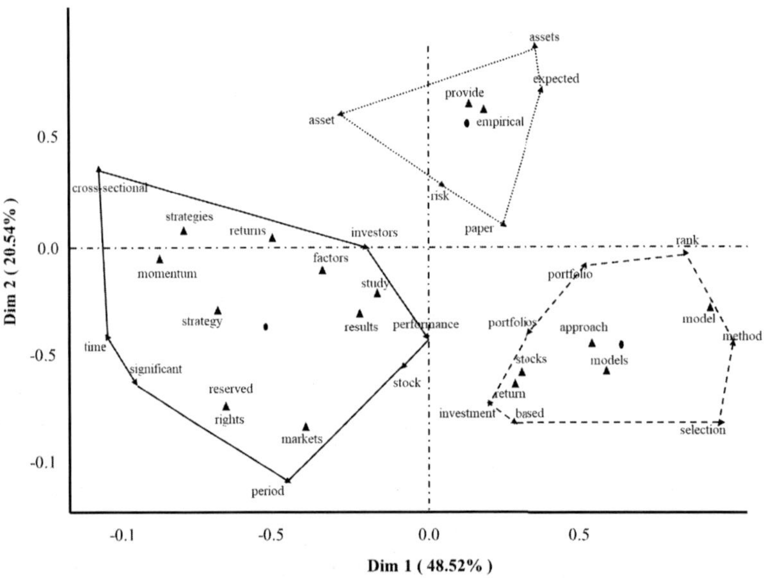

Source: Authors' own illustration based on biblioshiny BA analysis.

Figure 2. Map of Conceptual Structure.

Additionally, analysis of the bibliographic data revealed the most frequently used words in the titles of the retrieved documents for the period 1993 to 2024. For instance, among the 83 titles, the word "portfolio" had a frequency of 24, while the words "stock," "returns," and "cross-sectional" had frequencies of 13, 11, and 10, respectively. Figure 3 depicts the co-occurrence network in terms of the subject categories of the WoS database. As can be observed from Figure 3, business, finance, and economics were the top three subject categories to which the extracted bibliographic data belong. Moreover, the figure shows the multidisciplinary characteristic of the existing literature on the subject of interest.

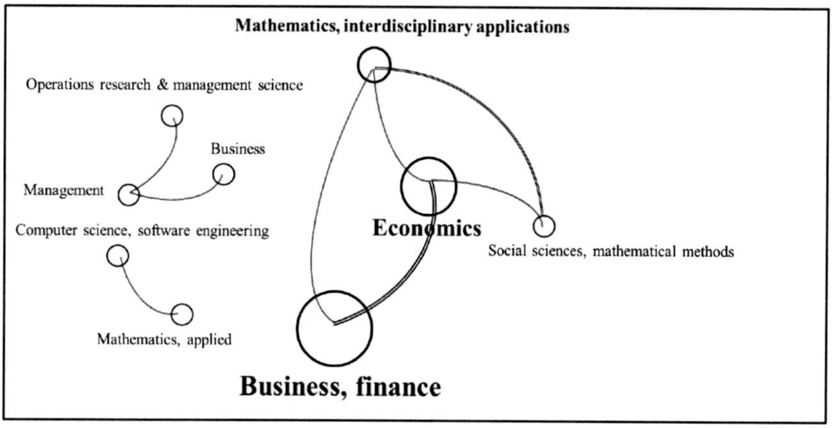

Source: Authors' own illustration based on biblioshiny BA analysis.

Figure 3. Co-Occurrence Network – WoS Subject Categories.

2.3.3. Analysis of Co-Citation and Collaboration

Co-citation analysis is a way to demonstrate the interconnections or interrelatedness among publications. The co-citation of two publications occurs when two documents are both cited in a third publication (Aria & Cuccurullo, 2017). Figure 4 presents the results of the co-citation analysis of the articles. As mentioned previously, the work by Jegadeesh and Titman (1993), the biggest node and named "jegadeesh n 1993" in Figure 4, was the most cited paper, obtaining 4618 citations globally. Overall, the works by Jegadeesh and Titman (1993), Carhart (1997), and Jegadeesh and Titman (2001) were identified as the most commonly co-citated papers on the subject.

Additionally, one of the most commonly employed ways of assessing the scientific outputs of researchers involves examining their collaboration network (CN). A scientific CN refers to a network with nodes showing the authors and links indicating the co-authorships (Glänzel & Schubert, 2004; Aria & Cuccurullo, 2017). According to the authors' CN analysis, Oh Kang Kwon and Stephen Satchell were the two authors who collaborated with the highest cumulative degree of one. When the collaboration between countries was considered, the frequency of collaboration between the UK and Australia was five. Collaboration between the USA and China also had a frequency of five. Moreover, the USA collaborated with the UK four times. The rest of the country collaborations with the USA had a frequency of one for each of the following countries: Canada, Hong Kong, India, Korea, Lebanon, and Singapore. By contrast, the collaboration frequency between China and the UK was four, while Australia had one collaboration with New Zealand. Furthermore, Canada collaborated with the USA, Finland, France, and Switzerland with a frequency of one each. Overall, among the 24 countries, the USA was the country with the highest frequency of collaboration.

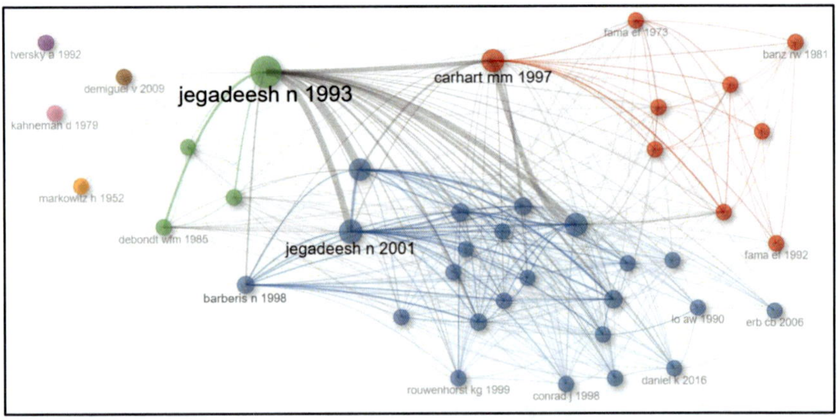

Source: Figure created by biblioshiny plug-in of the R software.

Figure 4. Co-Citation Network of Articles.

3. Rank-Based Portfolio Selection: Empirical Research

This section applies a recently proposed rank-based asset allocation strategy to an exchange-traded fund (ETF) portfolio and compares its results to those of several other portfolio allocation methods. The employed portfolio allocation strategy that uses the ranks of asset returns is called the *rank-based approach* (RBA) to portfolio asset allocation (Özgür & Sarıkovanlık, 2023). Moreover, the five different portfolio allocation methods employed, other than the RBA, are as follows: global minimum variance, global Min-CVaR, tangency, maximum diversification, and equally weighted portfolios. The portfolio asset allocation performance of these six different methods is assessed using several performance measures.

The following subsections first explain the characteristics of the ETF data and then provide definitions of the portfolio allocation strategies applied as well as the performance metrics employed. The final subsection reports and discusses the empirical findings.

3.1. Data

The daily price values of 11 ETFs are obtained from the finance.yahoo.com website for the period from January 5, 2015 to August 31, 2022. The logarithmic returns of the ETF series are estimated as follows:

$$r_{l,t} = \ln\left(P_{l,t} \,/\, P_{l,t-1}\right) \tag{3}$$

where $r_{l,t}$ is the return of ETF $l \in \{1,2, \dots ,, k\}$ estimated for the time (day) $t \in \{1,2, \dots , n\}$ and k is the total number of ETFs ($k = 11$). While $P_{l,t}$ refers to the price of ETF l obtained for day t, $P_{l,t-1}$ is the one-day lagged value of the price. Overall, 1929 daily returns are estimated for the ETF series. In other words, each ETF has 1929 return observations ($n = 1929$). Descriptive statistics concerning the estimated returns are provided in Table 3.

Table 3. Descriptives of the ETF Returns – Full Sample

ETF	Mean	Median	Minimum	Maximum	Standard Deviation	Skewness	Kurtosis
ASHR	-0.0001	0.0005	-0.2472	0.1829	0.0198	-1.0312	23.9606
DBC	0.0002	0.0010	-0.0828	0.0469	0.0116	-0.7997	7.8035
EWT	0.0003	0.0008	-0.1151	0.0653	0.0132	-0.8998	9.6577
GOVT	0.0000	0.0000	-0.0225	0.0223	0.0030	-0.1602	9.4587
IEFA	0.0000	0.0006	-0.1149	0.0809	0.0114	-1.4650	18.8187
QQQ	0.0006	0.0012	-0.1276	0.0813	0.0141	-0.6720	10.6972
SHY	0.0000	0.0000	-0.0051	0.0054	0.0008	-0.3265	10.1495
SJNK	-0.0001	0.0000	-0.0414	0.0569	0.0043	-0.3237	37.0937
SPIB	0.0000	0.0000	-0.0351	0.0472	0.0029	0.1320	70.8932
SPY	0.0003	0.0005	-0.1159	0.0867	0.0116	-0.9214	17.5057
VCIT	0.0000	0.0001	-0.0459	0.0529	0.0037	0.0494	44.4048

3.2. Methodology

This section employs six different portfolio selection methods. Among them, three have already been discussed in earlier chapters of this book. As a result, in this subsection, we only include very brief mathematical definitions of these portfolio allocation methods. A reader searching for deeper insight into the methods should consult the relevant chapters and the supplied references.

The first portfolio allocation strategy is the equally weighted or naïve portfolio. This is the portfolio in which an equal weight is assigned to each asset. As the ETF data consist of 11 return series, the weight of each portfolio constituent is estimated as in Equation 4.

$$w_l^{naive} = 1/k = 1/11, \text{ for } l \in \{1,2,\dots,k\} \tag{4}$$

The objective function of the global minimum variance (GMVP) portfolio optimization is defined as follows:

$$\min_{w \in S} \left[\boldsymbol{w}^T \, \Sigma \, \boldsymbol{w}\right] \tag{5}$$

In Equation 5, $\boldsymbol{w}$ is the vector of asset (the ETF in this case) weights, Σ represents the variance-covariance matrix, and S shows the set of feasible solutions, which is $S = \left\{\forall l = 1,2,\dots,k, w \in \mathbb{R}^k : \sum_{l=1}^{k} w_l = 1 \wedge w_l \geq 0\right\}$. The solution to Equation 5 yields an efficient portfolio with the smallest variance.

The tangency (TP) or maximum Sharpe portfolio is defined as follows (Sharpe, 1966; 1994):

$$\max_{w \in S} \left[\left(\boldsymbol{\mu}^T \boldsymbol{w} - r_f\right) / \sqrt{\boldsymbol{w}^T \, \Sigma \, \boldsymbol{w}} \right] \tag{6}$$

where $\boldsymbol{w}$, Σ, and S are defined as in the previous paragraphs. The term μ represents the vector of the ETF's mean returns and r_f is the risk-free rate. The solution to the maximization problem in Equation 6 yields a portfolio that has the maximum excess return per unit of portfolio risk assumed by an investor.

The objective of the global Min-CVaR portfolio is to minimize the portfolio CVaR value under a certain probability level of β:

$$\min_{w \in S} \left[CVaR_\beta(w)\right] \tag{7}$$

Rockafellar and Uryasev (2000) made a significant contribution to the literature by transforming the non-linear optimization shown in Equation 7 into an optimization with a linear objective function. In this framework, the mean–CVaR optimization problem does not require or assume elliptically distributed returns. By contrast, the MVOs shown in Equations 5 and 6 assume that the portfolio returns are elliptically distributed.

Another strategy employed in this chapter is the *maximum diversification* (maxDiv) portfolio reported by Choueifaty and Coignard (2008):

$$\max_{w \in S} \left[(\boldsymbol{w}^T \boldsymbol{\sigma}) \,/\, \sqrt{\boldsymbol{w}^T \, \Sigma \, \boldsymbol{w}} \right] \tag{8}$$

where $\boldsymbol{w}$, Σ, and S are defined as previously. The term $\boldsymbol{\sigma}$ is the vector of standard deviations of the asset (the ETFs in this case) returns.

The last portfolio allocation strategy is the RBA in portfolio asset allocation proposed by Özgür and Sarıkovanlık (2023):

$$\lambda_{l,t} = \begin{cases} exp(\mathcal{S}_{l,t}/n) \cdot exp(\mathcal{S}_{l,c}/k) \cdot r_{l,t} \; if \; r_{l,t} \geq 0 \\ \psi^2 \cdot exp(-\,\mathcal{S}_{l,t}/n) \cdot exp(-\,\mathcal{S}_{l,c}/k) \cdot r_{l,t} \; if \; r_{l,t} < 0 \end{cases} \tag{9}$$

In Equation 9, the term lambda $(\lambda_{l,t})$ is defined as the score of return l estimated for time $t \in \{1,2,\dots,n\}$. The term $\mathcal{S}_{l,t}$ represents the univariate rank of *t*th return among its own observations $\left(r_1^{[l]} \leq r_2^{[l]} \leq \cdots \leq r_n^{[l]}\right)$. Moreover, $\mathcal{S}_{l,c}$ is the cross-sectional rank of asset return l (in this case, the return of ETF l) observed at time t $\left(r_1^{[t]} \leq r_2^{[t]} \leq \cdots \leq r_l^{[t]}\right)$. Additionally, ψ^2 is defined as a tail parameter taking the value of one or four depending on the asset return and the tau threshold (τ) defined as follows:

$$\tau = q_{1\%}(Z) \wedge Z = \{q_{1\%}(r_1), q_{1\%}(r_2), \dots, q_{1\%}(r_l)\} \tag{10}$$

$$\psi^2 = \begin{cases} 1 \; if \; \tau \leq r_{l,t} < 0 \\ 4 \; if \; r_{l,t} < \tau < 0 \end{cases} \tag{11}$$

Following the estimation of the lambda, the one-period ahead portfolio weights of the assets are obtained as follows:

$$\widehat{w}_{l,t+1} = \left(\overline{w}_{\lambda_l} * \mathbb{I}_{\overline{w}>\mathbf{0}}\right) / \left(\textstyle\sum_{l=1}^{k} \overline{w}_{\lambda_l} * \mathbb{I}_{\overline{w}>\mathbf{0}}\right) \tag{12}$$

where $\widehat{w}_{l,t+1}$ is the one-period ahead portfolio allocation of the RBA for asset l and $\mathbb{I}_{\overline{w}>0}$ is the indicator function. Moreover, $\overline{w}_{\lambda_l}$ is the average of the in-sample relative weight $\left(w_{\lambda_{l,t}}\right)$ of return l estimated as follows:

$$w_{\lambda_{l,t}} = \lambda_{l,t} \,/\, \left|\sum_{l=1}^{k} \lambda_{l,t}\right| \;\wedge\; \overline{w}_{\lambda_l} = (1/n) * \sum_{t=1}^{n} w_{\lambda_{l,t}} \tag{13}$$

Similar to the GMVP, MinCVaR, TP, and maxDiv portfolios, the long-only $\left(\widehat{w}_{l,t+1} \geq 0\right)$ and full investment $\left(\sum_{l=1}^{k} \widehat{w}_{l,t+1} = 1\right)$ constraints are also applied in RBA portfolios. Furthermore, the out-sample portfolio allocations of all six strategies are estimated by using a one-period ahead rolling windows method with an in-sample size of 500.

3.3. Empirical Findings

Once the portfolio allocations of all the strategies (GMVP, Min-CVaR, TP, maxDiv, and RBA) are obtained, several portfolio metrics are estimated, including the return, risk, and return to variability ratios. Table 4 reports the estimated metrics of the portfolios constructed using the six different allocation methods. As can be inferred from Table 4, the portfolio constructed using the RBA had the highest mean return, Sharpe, and mean/semi-deviation (M/SD) ratios. The Sharpe ratio shows the obtained portfolio excess return per unit of portfolio risk. Here, we assumed the risk-free rate to be zero. The M/SD is the ratio of the portfolio return over the semi-deviation risk measure. While the Sharpe ratio employs the standard deviation as the measure of the portfolio risk, the M/SD ratio uses the semi-deviation risk measure. The difference between the standard deviation and the semi-deviation is that the former is a symmetric measure of both the upside and downside deviations from the mean, whereas the latter considers only the downside deviations from the mean or zero. As a result, semi-deviation does not evaluate the desired upside deviations (returns exceeding the mean) as part of the portfolio risk.

When the RBA portfolio is compared to the rest, the estimated Sharpe and mean/semi-deviation ratios indicate better performance in terms of the obtained portfolio return per unit of risk carried or assumed by the investor. Moreover, the second-best performer in terms of the portfolio return and return per unit of portfolio risk measures is the naïve or equally weighted portfolio. Indeed, in many cases in the finance literature, the naïve portfolio beat more sophisticated portfolio allocation methods or strategies.

Table 4. Performance Measures

Portfolio	Mean Return	Stand. Dev.	Semi Deviation	VaR% 1	Sharpe Ratio	Mean/Semi Deviation
Tangency	0.0141	0.7597	0.5767	2.4783	0.0185	0.0244
Min-CVaR	-0.0013	0.0801	0.0611	0.2745	-0.0168	-0.0220
Naive portf.	0.0159	0.6239	0.4823	1.6547	0.0256	0.0331
RBA	0.0193	0.5864	0.4275	1.8157	0.0328	0.0450
GMVP	-0.0009	0.0788	0.0600	0.2716	-0.0113	-0.0148
maxDiv	0.0015	0.1630	0.1254	0.5483	0.0091	0.0118

Additionally, the GMVP obtained the best values (the smallest values) for each portfolio risk measure—namely, the portfolio standard deviation, semi-deviation, and VaR—at the 99% confidence level. When compared with the global Min-CVaR portfolio, the GMVP also yielded better values in terms of the portfolio return and return per unit of portfolio risk metrics.

4. Discussion and Conclusion

In this chapter, we first introduced the fundamentals of ranks, RS, and bibliometrics. Then, we systematically analyzed the literature on the applications of ranks and/or RS in the portfolio allocation context from 1993 to 2024. We searched for and extracted relevant literature from the WoS database. Following a thorough examination and data cleaning step, we utilized the biblioshiny plug-in of the R software to analyze the bibliographic data. According to the results obtained, there were 83 documents published in 63 different sources, with an annual growth rate of 8.35%. We identified Jegadeesh and Titman (1993), Hartzmark (2015), and Dorfleitner et al. (2020) as the top three most frequently cited documents. Moreover, Oh Kang Kwon, Stephen Satchell, and Zuo Quan Xu were the top three most relevant authors. The University of Sydney, Hong Kong Polytechnic University, and Columbia University were the most prominent affiliations. Among the 24 countries, the USA, China, and the UK were the top three countries based on the total number of publications on the subject.

Nevertheless, it is also important to note the limitations of the BA applied in this chapter, which only employed bibliographic data retrieved from the WoS database. We chose the WoS for the analysis because of its data quality and detailed records of the document attributes, some of which were missing in other databases. However, a more extensive BA of the literature could be conducted by employing other scientific databases. Moreover, we only considered documents published in English. As a result, scientific works published in other languages are not reflected in the results. Additionally, we employed only two types of documents in the analysis—that is, book chapters and both early access and review articles. Overall, BA is a trending and excellent method of analyzing a large number of scientific outputs of researchers, institutions, and/or countries. However, as noted by Yıldız and Karakuş Yılmaz (2023) and Rashid (2023), researchers need to be careful when selecting search keywords and apply a data cleaning step so that their BA is not affected by various kinds of data-specific errors.

The final section of this chapter applied a recently proposed rank-based method—namely, the RBA—in a portfolio asset allocation task. The portfolio constituents were 11 different ETFs with a time span of over seven years of daily data. The portfolio allocation performance of the RBA was compared to that of the GMVP, global Min-CVaR, tangency, maxDiv, and naïve portfolios by using the portfolio return, risk, and return per unit of the variability ratios. In summary, the estimated performance metrics indicate the superior performance of the RBA in terms of the return and return per unit of risk measures. If the desired outcome is to minimize the portfolio risk independent of the return or return-related measures, the GMVP yielded the lowest portfolio risk for each estimated metric.

References

Aria, M., & Cuccurullo, C. (2017). bibliometrix: An R-tool for Comprehensive Science Mapping Analysis. *Journal of Informetrics*, *11*(4), 959–975. https://doi.org/10.1016/j.joi.2017.08.007.

Bahoo, S., Cucculelli, M., Goga, X., & Mondolo, J. (2024). Artificial Intelligence in Finance: A Comprehensive Review through Bibliometric and Content Analysis. *SN Business & Economics*, *4*(2), 23. https://doi.org/10.1007/s43546-023-00618-x.

Campbell, F. (1896). *The Theory of National and International Bibliography: With Special Reference to the Introduction of System in the Record of Modern Literature*. Library Bureau.

Carhart, M. M. (1997). On Persistence in Mutual Fund Performance. *The Journal of Finance*, *52*(1), 57–82.

Chen, X., & Xiang, S. (2016). Sparse Solutions of Linear Complementarity Problems. *Mathematical Programming*, *159*, 539–556. https://doi.org/10.1007/s10107-015-0950-x.

Choueifaty, Y., & Coignard, Y. (2008). Toward Maximum Diversification. *The Journal of Portfolio Management*, *35*(1), 40–51. https://doi.org/10.3905/JPM.2008.35.1.40.

Costa, D. F., Carvalho, F. M., Moreira, B. C. M., & Prado, J. W. (2017). Bibliometric Analysis on the Association between Behavioral Finance and Decision Making with Cognitive Biases such as Overconfidence, Anchoring Effect and Confirmation Bias. *Scientometrics*, *111*(3), 1775–1799. https://doi.org/10.1007/s11192-017-2371-5.

Costa, D. F., Carvalho, F. d. M., & Moreira, B. C. d. M. (2019). Behavioral Economics and Behavioral Finance: A Bibliometric Analysis of the Scientific Fields. *Journal of Economic Surveys*, *33*, 3–24. https://doi.org/10.1111/joes.12262.

David, H. A. (2006). Topics in the History of Order Statistics. In N. Balakrishnan, E. Castillo, & J. M. Sarabia (Eds.) *Advances in Distribution Theory, Order Statistics, and Inference* (pp.157–172). Springer Science & Business Media.

David, H. A., & Nagaraja, H. N. (2006). Order Statistics. In S. Kotz (Ed.) *Encyclopedia of Statistical Sciences* (2nd ed., Vol. 9, pp.5829–5838). John Wiley & Sons.

Donaldson, J., Flagg, D., & Hunter Orr, J. (2011). Selecting Stocks and Building Portfolios: A Sorting Exercise. *Managerial Finance*, *37*(7), 636–646. https://doi.org/10.1108/03074351111140270.

Dorfleitner, G., Kreuzer, C., & Sparrer, C. (2020). ESG Controversies and Controversial ESG: About Silent Saints and Small Sinners. *Journal of Asset Management*, *21*, 393–412. https://doi.org/10.1057/s41260-020-00178-x.

Dragulescu, A., & Arendt, C. (2020). _xlsx: Read, Write, Format Excel 2007 and Excel 97/2000/XP/2003 Files_. R package version 0.6.5. https://CRAN.R-project.org/package=xlsx.

Ge, Y., Chao, T., Sun, J., Liu, W., Chen, Y., & Wang, C. (2022). Frontiers and Hotspots Evolution in Psycho-Cardiology: A Bibliometric Analysis from 2004 to 2022. *Current Problems in Cardiology*, *47*(12), 101361. https://doi.org/10.1016/j.cpcardiol.2022.101361.

Glänzel, W., & Schubert, A. (2004). Analysing Scientific Networks Through Co-Authorship. In H. F. Moed, W. Glänzel, & U. Schmoch (Eds.) *Handbook of Quantitative Science and Technology Research.* Springer. https://doi.org/10.1007/1-4020-2755-9_12.

Ham, H., Cho, H., Kim, H., & Ryu, D. (2019). Time-series Momentum in China's Commodity Futures Market. *Journal of Futures Markets*, *39*, 1515–1528. https://doi.org/10.1002/fut.22053.

Hartzmark, S. M. (2015). The Worst, the Best, Ignoring All the Rest: The Rank Effect and Trading Behavior. *The Review of Financial Studies*, *28*(4), 1024–1059. https://doi.org/10.1093/rfs/hhu079.

Hood, W., & Wilson, C. S. (2001). The Literature of Bibliometrics, Scientometrics, and Informetrics. *Scientometrics*, *52*(2), 291–314.

Hulme E. W. (1923). *Statistical Bibliography in Relation to the Growth of Modern Civilization.* Grafton.

Jegadeesh, N, & Titman, S. (1993). Returns to Buying Winners and Selling Losers: Implications for Stock Market Efficiency. *The Journal of Finance*, *48*, 65–91. https://doi.org/10.1111/j.1540-6261.1993.tb04702.x.

Jegadeesh, N., & Titman, S. (2001). Profitability of Momentum Strategies: An Evaluation of Alternative Explanations. *The Journal of Finance*, *56*(2), 699–720.

Kendall, M. G. (1962). *Rank Correlation Methods*. Hafner.

Kwon, O. K., & Satchell, S. (2024). Statistical Properties of Co-quantiles and their Applications to Momentum Spillovers. *Communications in Statistics - Theory and Methods*, *53*(20), 7332–7351. https://doi.org/10.1080/03610926.2023.2263116.

Lawani, S. M. (1981). Bibliometrics: Its Theoretical Foundations, Methods and Applications. *Libri*, *31*(4), 294-315. https://doi.org/10.1515/libr.1981.31.1.294.

Liu, M. Liu, Q., & MA, T. (2011). The 52-Week High Momentum Strategy in International Stock Markets. *Journal of International Money and Finance*, *30*(1), 180–204. https://doi.org/10.1016/j.jimonfin.2010.08.004.

Liu, W. S., Gu, M. D., Hu, G. Y., Li, C., Liao, H. C., Tang, L., & Shapira, P. (2014). Profile of Developments in Biomass-based Bioenergy Research: a 20-year Perspective. *Scientometrics*, *99*(2), 507–521. https://doi.org/10.1007/s11192-013-1152-z.

Nalimov, W., & Mulchenko, B. M. (1969). *Naukometriya* [*Scientometrics*]. Nauka.

Osareh, F. (1996). Bibliometrics, Citation Analysis and Co-Citation Analysis: A Review of Literature I. *Libri*, *46*(3), 149–158. https://doi.org/10.1515/libr.1996.46.3.149.

Özgür, C., & Sarikovanlik, V. (2023): A Rank-Based Approach in Portfolio Asset Allocation. *Applied Economics Letters, 31*(20), 2223–2227. https://doi.org/10.1080/13504851.2023.2212961.

Özgür, C., & Sarıkovanlık, V. (2024). *Univariate and Cross-Sectional Ranks of Asset Returns: Are They Relevant to Portfolio Allocation?* Generis Publishing.

Qudah, H., Baqila, B. K. A., Albadienah, J. M. O., AlQudah, M. Z., Al Qudah, S., Alrahamneh, S., Ababne, A., & Qudah, I. (2024). Using Bibliometrics to Understand Algorithmic Finance. *Journal of Applied Economics*, *27*(1), 2389497. https://doi.org/10.1080/15140326.2024.2389497.

Patari, E., Leivo, T., & Honkapuro, S. (2012). Enhancement of Equity Portfolio Performance using Data Envelopment Analysis. *European Journal of Operational Research*, *220*(3), 786–797. https://doi.org/10.1016/j.ejor.2012.02.006.

Prado, J. W., Alcantara, V. D., Carvalho, F. D., Vieira, K. C., Machado, L. K. C., & Tonelli, D. F. (2016). Multivariate Analysis of Credit Risk and Bankruptcy Research Data: A Bibliometric Study Involving Different Knowledge Fields (1968–2014). *Scientometrics*, *106*(3), 1007–1029. https://doi.org/10.1007/s11192-015-1829-6.

Pritchard, A. (1969). Statistical Bibliography or Bibliometrics? *Journal of Documentation*, *25*(4), 348–349.

Qasim, M. (2017). Sustainability and Wellbeing: A Scientometric and Bibliometric Review of the Literature. *Journal of Economic Surveys*, *31*(4), 1035–1061. https://doi.org/10.1111/joes.12183.

R Core Team (2023). R: A Language and Environment for Statistical Computing. R Foundation for Statistical Computing, Vienna, Austria. https://www.R-project.org/.

Ranganathan, S. R. (1948). *Proceedings of the Aslib's Annual Conference*. Leamington Spa, Great Britain.

Rashid, M. F. A. (2023). How to Conduct a Bibliometric Analysis using R Packages: A Comprehensive Guidelines. *Journal of Tourism, Hospitality & Culinary Arts*, *15*(1), 24–39.

Rockafellar, R. T., & Uryasev, S. (2000). Optimization of Conditional Value-at-Risk. *Journal of Risk*, *2*, 21–42.

Salini, S. (2016). An Introduction to Bibliometrics. In T. Greenfield, & S. Greener (Eds.) *Research Methods for Postgraduates* (pp. 130–143). John Wiley & Sons, Ltd. https://doi.org/10.1002/9781118763025.ch14.

Secinaro, S., Calandra, D., Petricean, D., Chmet, F. (2021). Social Finance and Banking Research as a Driver for Sustainable Development: A Bibliometric Analysis. *Sustainability*, *13*, 330. https://doi.org/10.3390/su13010330.

Sen, P. K. (2006). Rank Statistics. In S. Kotz (Ed.) *Encyclopedia of Statistical Sciences* (2nd ed., Vol. 10, pp. 6922–6932). John Wiley & Sons, Ltd.

Sengupta, I. N. (1992). Bibliometrics, Informetrics, Scientometrics and Librametrics: An Overview. *Libri*, *42*(2), 75–98. https://doi.org/10.1515/libr.1992.42.2.75.

Sharpe, W. F. (1966). Mutual Fund Performance. *The Journal of Business*, *39*(1), 119–138.

Sharpe, W. F. (1994). The Sharpe Ratio. *The Journal of Portfolio Management*, *21*(1), 49–58. https://doi.org/10.3905/jpm.1994.409501.

Song, Q., Liu, A., & Yang, S. Y. (2017). Stock Portfolio Selection using Learning-to-Rank Algorithms with News Sentiment. *Neurocomputing*, 264, 20–28. https://doi.org/10.1016/j.neucom.2017.02.097.

Taniguchi, M., Shiraishi, H., Hirukawa, J., Solvang, H. K., & Yamashita, T. (2018). *Statistical Portfolio Estimation*. Chapman and Hall/CRC.

Tse, Y. (2015). Momentum Strategies with Stock Index Exchange-traded Funds. *The North American Journal of Economics and Finance*, *33*, 134–148. https://doi.org/10.1016/j.najef.2015.04.003.

Wilcoxon, F. (1945). Individual Comparisons by Ranking Methods. *Biometrics Bulletin*, *1*(6), 80–83.

Xu, Z. Q. (2016), A Note on the Quantile Formulation. *Mathematical Finance*, *26*, 589–601. https://doi.org/10.1111/mafi.12072.

Yıldız, M., & Karakuş Yılmaz, T. (2023). Bibliometric Analysis in Scientific Research using R: A Review of Scopus and Web of Science Databases. *Journal of Data Applications*, *2*, 31–46. https://doi.org/10.26650/JODA.1462396.

Zhou, W., Luo, D., Fang, H., Gou, X., & Chen, J. (2020). Bibliometric Overview and Retrospective Analysis of Fund Performance Research between 1966 and 2019. *Economic research-Ekonomska istraživanja*, *33*(1), 1510–1537. https://doi.org/10.1080/1331677X.2020.1755879.

Chapter 5

Asset Allocation in Times of Machines: A Review of the Methods and Applications

Cemile Özgür*, **PhD**
Department of Management Information Systems, Boğaziçi University, Istanbul, Türkiye

Abstract

This chapter begins with a brief introduction to the fundamentals of machine learning, which defines and explains the terms commonly employed in the literature. This will help the reader to grasp the findings and corresponding arguments from various studies discussed in the field as well as in the following sections of this chapter. The second section introduces the four main types of machine learning frequently mentioned in the literature. The aim here is to help the reader differentiate and choose from among the various machine learning algorithms, depending on the data and the learning task they want to accomplish. The third section provides a brief overview of the applications of machine learning in the finance sector, such as the pricing of financial assets, algorithmic trading, managing financial risks, developing financial technologies, detecting fraud, modeling investor behavior, and conducting sentiment analysis. Moreover, it reports on over 100 examples of published work related to the various applications of machine learning in the finance sector. Section four focuses on asset allocation and reviews various articles that utilize machine learning algorithms in portfolio selection tasks. Finally, the fifth section discusses the challenges of employing machine learning as well as the field's future research prospects. Overall, this chapter aids the reader first by introducing the fundamental concepts of machine learning and then by offering a comprehensive literature

* Corresponding Author's Email: cemile.ozgur@pt.bogazici.edu.tr / ozgurcemile@yahoo.com

In: Title
Editors: Name
ISBN:

review that evaluates over 150 published academic works discussing the field of machine learning or using algorithms in relation to various finance-related topics.

Keywords: Machine learning, stock markets, financial applications, asset allocation, deep learning

1. Basic Concepts

The term *machine learning* refers to a set of computational algorithms developed to mimic human learning. While human learning entails a complex process acquired by observing the environment and analyzing the inputs that lead to the development of new or modified skills, knowledge, or behaviors, computational algorithms are designed to learn from data by repetition or experience so that they can adapt their structure to achieve a specified or desired outcome. The background to this concept dates back to the seventeenth century, when Pascal and Leibniz developed machines that could add or subtract numbers (El Naqa & Murphy, 2015). Moreover, McCulloch and Pitts's (1943) idea of mimicking the human brain by applying logic and designing computational networks similar to the neural activities of biological neurol networks paved the way for the development of artificial neural networks (Carbonell et al. 1983). However, it was Arthur Samuel who introduced the term machine learning in 1959. In his seminal publication, Samuel (1959) defined machine learning as a field of study consisting of the procedures for programming computers to learn by playing a game or experiencing a specific task so that explicit or additional programming is not necessary. Samuel (1959) used the game of checkers to show that a computer can be programmed to learn, and with sufficient repetition (experience), can also beat or perform better than its programmer. Additionally, he argued that his example can be applied to many different situations.

Another milestone in the development of machine learning (ML) was the invention of *perceptrons* in 1957. As defined by Rosenblatt (1957, 1962), the term perceptron refers to the simplest neural network structure that uses a threshold activation function (Bishop, 1995). Nevertheless, the field of ML did not show much progress until the 1980s. Indeed, while the *k-nearest neighbor* (kNN) algorithm was originally developed in 1951 (Fix & Hodges, 1989), research in the field of ML was accelerated by the development of perceptrons with many layers, which are called *multilayer perceptrons*

(MLPs) or *artificial neural networks* (ANNs). The development of the multilayer perceptron was followed by proposals for *decision trees* in 1986 (Quinlan, 1986) and *support vector machines* in 1995 (Cortes & Vapnik, 1995). Furthermore, *ensemble methods*, which were described by Zhou (2012) as *committee-based learning* algorithms for training multiple (or a set of) learners to achieve a specific outcome, as well as *relevance vector machines* (Tipping, 2001) represent the other significant contributions to the field. Additionally, the integration of non-linear kernel activation functions into the ANN structure was another important step in the development of ML and its applications, since it enhanced the scope of applications of the ANN algorithm. In the twenty-first century, the research on ANN algorithms with deeper structures has been accelerated due to technological developments and increased computational power. Due to technological advancements, researchers were able to develop and use more complex neural network structures consisting of many layers and neurons, which is referred to as *deep learning*, for example, *recurrent neural networks* and *convolutional neural networks*. As a result, recent research on deep learning, which has been growing as a subfield of ML, includes various developments and/or applications of different types of deep neural networks. Still, since this chapter cannot cover all the developments in the constantly evolving field of ML, the following paragraphs will differentiate the two commonly employed terms of *artificial intelligence* and ML by putting them in context and supplying the overall frame so that the reader's understanding of these concepts is enhanced.

While the terms ML and artificial intelligence might be used interchangeably, leading to incorrect definitions and/or confusion among the concepts, ML is actually a subfield of artificial intelligence and sits at the intersection of various disciplines, such as probability and computational statistics, information theory, psychology, neuroscience, and mathematical optimization. As previously explained, ML concerns computer programs that can learn a task or behavior for a specific purpose in order to produce a desired outcome without the need for explicit programming. According to Mitchell (1997), who is frequently quoted with his definition of "learning" of ML:

> "A computer program is said to learn from experience E with respect to some class of tasks T and performance measure P, if its performance at tasks in T, as measured by P, improves with experience E."

In this sense, the behavior or task is learned based on three main factors: (a) the data set that is used by the program, (b) a metric or error measure quantifying the distance between the desired outcome and the observed (actual) outcome, and (c) an adjustment mechanism that uses the distance measure or estimated error metric to supply feedback and guide the program for the purpose of obtaining outcomes closer to the desired ones. As mentioned by Joshi (2023), the field of ML consists of the methods and learning algorithms necessary to construct *artificially intelligent* mechanisms.

By contrast, artificial intelligence (AI), as the overall category that includes ML, has a broader definition that refers to the intelligent systems capable of imitating human behavior or thinking. As noted by Manyika (2022), there are various definitions of AI, with the recent trend being to associate any research consisting of not only ML but also automation, algorithms, and data science with AI. However, it is possible to classify the definitions of AI into two main types. The first type defines AI as an artificial system, a robot, or a computer that can conduct tasks belonging to intelligent beings, such as the speech recognition, reasoning, visual perception, decision-making, and learning abilities of human beings. The second type defines AI as an artificial system with the ability to perceive or comprehend its surroundings and take actions to maximize the probability of attaining goals that are either given externally or set via self-learning (Poole et al. 1998; Manyika, 2022).

Moreover, Soori et al. (2023) proposed a clear task-based differentiation of AL and ML in the field of advanced robotic systems. According to Soori et al. (2023), while AI enables researchers or developers to create robots with abilities that mimic human-like behavior, such as perceiving the environment (surroundings), making judgements, and acting autonomously, ML is employed to improve the performance of the created robots by enabling them to learn from data or their experiences. AI was first developed in 1955 through the attempts of John McCarthy, Marvin Minsky, Claude Shannon, and Nathaniel Rochester, who proposed the *Dartmouth Workshop* (McCarthy et al. 1955). Until the 1990s, the field of AI was dominated by inductive logic programming and knowledge-based systems, which depend on logic and tasks defined with symbolic representations. However, the accelerated developments in terms of ML shifted the field toward data-driven approaches that use big data (a large amount of data) to train computers, identify patterns, and obtain desired outcomes (Wang et al. 2020). Figure 1 shows the overall category of AI together with its subfields.

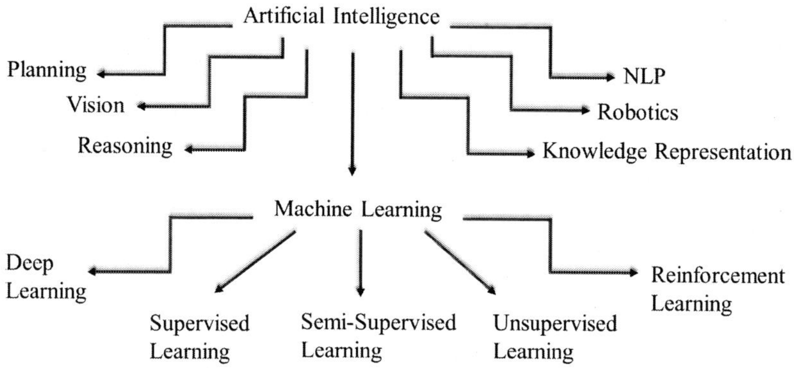

Source: Author's own illustration.

Figure 1. Artificial Intelligence and Its Subfields.

As can be seen in Figure 1, AI is a superset of ML, as are the others, such as *naturel language processing* (NLP), *knowledge representation, robotics, vision, reasoning*, and *planning* (Russel & Norvig, 2020; Gupta et al. 2021). As this chapter focuses on ML and its applications in asset allocation, it does not go into detail concerning the other subsets of AI. However, the reader can consult the supplied references and other books focused on AI, for example, the book by Russel and Norvig (2020), for deeper knowledge and discussion of the subject.

2. Forms of Machine Learning

ML algorithms are classified into various types depending on the data and the learning task that the user aims to accomplish. As mentioned in the previous section, ML requires data to learn a task or behavior. If there is data with an output set of *finite* or *categorical values* (such as true/false, like/dislike, or rainy/sunny/cloudy), then the type of learning is termed *classification*. In this case, ML algorithms group or categorize the data into certain classes by predicting their probability. Conversely, if there is numerical data (a real number or an integer) with which ML algorithms can produce *numeric predictions* of the output set, then the type of learning is termed *regression*. As explained by Russel and Norvig (2020), a better name for this type of learning would have been *numerical prediction* or *function approximation*, since the statistical method of regression to the mean is not what is being referred to here. Currently, the field of ML covers a wide range of algorithms for decision making, predictions, and pattern recognition. As a result, there are many ML algorithms that can be used in regression (numerical prediction) or classification tasks, including the least absolute shrinkage and selection operator (LASSO), nearest neighbors, support vector machines (SVM), random forests and various types of recently developed neural networks.

In ML terminology, a set of data used by an algorithm is called *training data*. The process of feeding the training data to an algorithm so that it can identify the existing patterns and adjust its parameters to accomplish the desired task is described as *training* the ML model rather than the learning of the model. However, the ML algorithm itself is often referred to as the *learner*. It is possible to differentiate learners into four main learning forms—namely, *supervised learning*, *unsupervised learning*, *semi-supervised learning*, and *reinforcement learning*. As noted by Emmert-Streib et al. (2023), there are also other learning forms that researchers have termed the *modern learning paradigms*, such as *transfer learning*, *one-class classification*, *multi-task learning*, *few/one-shot learning*, *multi-label learning*, and *positive-unlabeled learning*. Nevertheless, the following subsections briefly define and focus on the four main learning forms that are well positioned in the current ML literature.

2.1. Supervised Learning

In this form of learning, the training data set consists of input data as well as a set of outputs. In the ML literature, the input data set is called the *attribute* or *feature set*, while the set of outputs is often referred to as the *response* (*target*) *variables* or *labels*. In *supervised learning* (SL), the ML algorithm, which is fed with the input–output data pairs, infers a function that can map from the input variables (features) to the outputs (labels) with a precision that is as close as possible to the true function. Here, the term supervised refers to the supervisory role of the labels that show the algorithm the task it is expected to learn. More formally, let us assume that we have a set of T samples of input–output pairs with $\mathcal{X} = \{x_1, \ldots, x_t\}$ representing the input set and $\mathcal{Y} = \{y_1, \ldots, y_t\}$ denoting the output set.

$$\mathcal{Y} = f(\mathcal{X}) \tag{1}$$

As shown in Equation 1, SL algorithms infer and use a function $(f(.))$ to predict the labels $(y_1, \ldots, y_t)$ by employing the features $(x_1, \ldots, x_t)$ given in the training data. The aim is to find the function $\hat{f}(\mathcal{X})$ that approximates to the real one $(f(\mathcal{X}))$ defining the predictive relation between the input–output data pairs. In other words, the aim is to develop a regressor or classifier that will be able to estimate the response variables for the previously unseen data, which is called *test data*. If an algorithm is employed to predict a numeric target value, then it is used in a regression task, as explained previously. By contrast, if an algorithm is employed to predict the probability of a categorical response variable, then it is used in a classification task. In the classification task, $f: \mathcal{X} \to \mathcal{G}$, where $\mathcal{G} \in \mathcal{C} := \{0, \ldots, \mathcal{C} - 1\}$, $\hat{\mathcal{G}}$ denotes the predictor, and $\mathcal{C}$ refers to the number of categories (Dixon et al. 2020). Moreover, an SL algorithm used in regression tasks might not be employed in classification tasks, and vice versa. However, most SL algorithms can be used in both classification and regression tasks.

As stated by Dixon et al. (2020), an SL algorithm can also be classified as either a generative or discriminative model. An SL model that is an implicit learner of the distribution of the response (output) variables, depending on the inputs, is referred to as discriminative, such as a neural network, whereas an explicit learner of the joint distribution of the response and input variables represents the generative class of SL algorithms, such as a *restricted Boltzmann machine*.

2.2. Unsupervised Learning

Unsupervised learning (UL) refers to the form of learning without supervisors, since UL algorithms use data without a set of outputs. In other words, the training data set in UL is composed of only the inputs without any correspondence to the output data. As a result, an ML algorithm fed with data without labels tries to identify *groups* and/or *associations* among the data. The identified groups may be either specific *clusters*, known as *clustering*, or specific inputs, leaving out the unnecessary ones to *reduce dimensionality*.

In the case of clustering, the goal is to segment a set of observations into groups based on some similar patterns or characteristics without knowing the inherent groupings in the observed data. Data clustering is commonly used by both academics and industry experts. Linear discriminant analysis, Gaussian mixture models, hierarchical clustering, and *k*-means clustering are among the frequently applied clustering algorithms. While researchers in academia can use clustering in exploratory research, industry experts can apply it to identify groups of customers or companies with similar credit risk, trading, and/or purchasing behavior.

By contrast, dimensionality reduction (DR) aims to identify and extract a set of inputs with some statistical regularities or even irregularities. DR is an important concept in the ML literature because an increase in dimensionality might also increase the complexity of an ML model, leading to difficulty in its application. However, it is also important to note that DR might lead to a decrease in the accuracy of an ML model. As a result, it involves a tradeoff between model accuracy and simplicity, which leads to more efficient and faster ML applications. Examples of frequently applied DR algorithms include self-organizing maps, multidimensional scaling, and principal component analysis (Hastie et al. 2009).

2.3. Semi-Supervised Learning

The learning of ML algorithms is also differentiated into a *semi-supervised learning* (SSL) form whereby some of the response variables or labels of the training data are missing. Not every feature in the training data matches a label, and the number of output observations is smaller than the number of corresponding features. In this case, together with the outputs, the features are used to infer information for the purpose of constructing a learner with better performance than the learners constructed using only the data with labels. As a result, SSL stands at the intersection of SL and UL due to using both when necessary. Currently, there are many SSL methods, for example, the generative models, self-training methods, graph-based methods, and hybrid methods. The reader can consult the works of Hady and Schwenker (2013), van Engelen and Hoos (2020), and Yang et al. (2023) to acquire deeper knowledge on this subject.

2.4. Reinforcement Learning

Reinforcement learning (RL) refers to the form of learning that sequentially decides on actions in response to a dynamic environment for the purpose of maximizing the overall reward. In other words, the learning process and actions of RL algorithms are based on sequential assessments of interactions with the environment that yield feedback (a reward) for each action taken at a specific time step and in a specific state. As a result, RL is a dynamic type of learning that can more closely mimic the actual biological process of learning.

The learning forms explored in the preceding subsections—that is, SL, SSL, and UL—are differentiated depending on the availability of labeled data. The algorithms that use one of these forms of learning assume that a data set is already available for their use, and they do not need a dynamic interaction with the environment. As mentioned by Joshi (2023), they can be referred to as *offline* methods. Conversely, RL has an active learning approach that fundamentally differs from the rest (SL, SSL, and UL) and so can be referred to as an *online* learning method.

3. An Overview of Machine Learning in Finance

Recent technological developments have enabled researchers and industry experts to successfully utilize ML algorithms in a wide range of industrial applications and in various fields of academic research. Çelik and Altunaydın (2018) highlighted that education is one of the most significant fields of application of ML. Moreover, it is possible to find different applications of ML in the fields of law, medicine, agriculture, computational biology, archeology, meteorology, economics, and finance, as well as in other scientific fields not mentioned here.

Finance is one of the most important fields of application of ML. Over the last fifty years, the accelerated developments in the field have opened the doors to complex and high-capacity computations that could barely have been imagined before and resulted in a revolutionary effect on the scientific field of finance and on the finance sector and its practices. Currently, several tasks undertaken by finance professionals and academic researchers are carried out by employing various ML algorithms. ML algorithms are also employed in various services in the banking sector, as well as in other financial institutions, such as anti-money laundering operations, virtual assistants, regulatory services, and so on. It is important to note here that the terms AI and ML are used interchangeably in some published academic research and in industry practices in the finance sector.

The following subsections explain the main applications of ML in different subfields of finance and discuss some of the related academic research. However, the reader should keep in mind that the intention of this chapter is not to cover all the applications of ML in the field of finance, given that it is possible to find a vast amount of academic research on the subject. For instance, a Google Scholar search using the keywords "machine learning" and "finance" yielded 963,000 results in November 2024. Similarly, Scopus and Web of Science (all databases) searches using the same keywords resulted with 23,523 and 10,602 items of published academic research, respectively.

3.1. Asset Pricing

One fundamental task in finance is the valuation or pricing of a financial asset, such as a stock, bond, or derivative. The contribution of ML to this core field of finance is highly significant for several reasons. One such reason, which is termed the *high-dimensionality problem*, is the inability of traditional statistical methods (e.g., ordinary least squares [OLS]) to produce useful forecasts (forecasts of excess returns, cash flows, etc.) when the number of explanatory or predictor variables exceeds the number of observations. Another issue when using traditional statistical methods arises when the associations among the predicted or dependent variables and the predictor variables are overly complex and non-linear. Conversely, ML algorithms can successfully produce predictions under high dimensionality as well as with complex and non-linear associations. The prediction tasks of excess returns in asset pricing and cash flows in asset valuation models can be performed using the supervised ML algorithms discussed earlier in this chapter.

Asset pricing is a highly active subfield of study in terms of finance. As a result, it is possible to find many published studies using different types of ML algorithms in various prediction tasks within the asset pricing literature. The works by Yao et al. (2000), Culkin and Das (2017), Weigand (2019), Gu et al. (2020), Bianchi et al. (2021), Gu et al. (2021), Giglio et al. (2022), and Fallahgoul et al. (2024) are examples of published academic research focusing on ML and asset pricing. Moreover, Ozbayoglu et al. (2020), and Olorunnimbe and Viktor (2023) supplied extensive reviews of deep learning applications in asset pricing and finance in general.

Academic researchers might obtain return forecasts for assets to test the asset pricing models. Financial experts might use such predictions to identify underpriced or overpriced assets so that the buy, hold, or sell signals of the assets can be produced. However, as noted by Nagel (2021), most of the time, the main purpose of price or return predictions is to construct a portfolio. Thus, the next section of this chapter, which focuses on the applications of ML algorithms in portfolio asset allocation, also considers research on asset pricing with ML that is conditional on the next step of constructing a portfolio using at least one of several portfolio selection strategies.

3.2. Algorithmic Trading

Algorithmic trading (AT) refers to the buy and sell decisions or orders of computer algorithms (algorithmic models) with predefined trading instructions that depend on the time, price, or volume of the assets. The ability of ML algorithms to handle vast amounts of data (big data comprising historical and/or real-time observations), as well as their capability for high-accuracy pattern recognition and prediction, has led to them being increasingly employed in trading strategies. Moreover, recent developments in electronic trading platforms have facilitated the utilization of AT strategies. AT can be narrowly defined as the trading orders of computers with partial or no human interaction that mostly rely on the future price, volume, and/or volatility predictions of the ML algorithms yielding the trading signals (buy/sell decisions) for assets based on the predefined instructions.

According to Treleaven et al. (2013), the AT volume of American equities was greater than 73% of all the traded volume in 2011. Furthermore, Treleaven et al. (2013) mentioned several key operating stages of AT, such as the pre-trade analysis, generation of the trading signal, execution of the trade, and post-trade analysis. Hu et al. (2015) conducted a literature review on the applications of evolutionary computation methods in the discovery of rules concerning the AT of stocks. Additionally, Virgilio (2019) reviewed the literature on high-frequency trading and assessed its impact on financial crises and market quality in terms of liquidity, volatility, price discovery, and costs of transactions. Özgür and Sarıkovanlık (2022) proposed unique hybrid ML algorithms and employed them to predict the returns of two stock indices, the BIST100 and NASDAQ. Moreover, Özgür and Sarıkovanlık (2022) developed a trading strategy based on the return forecasts of the employed single and hybrid ML algorithms to evaluate the economic impact of the forecasting agents. Sahu et al. (2023) grouped the AT of stocks into six trading strategies—namely, trend following, momentum trading, mean reversion, breakout, moving average crossover, and statistical arbitrage strategies. More recently, Khan and Hassan (2024) proposed an AT algorithm that employs decimated data to decrease the complexity and computational needs of AT strategies. The reader can consult the works by Wang and Yan (2021) and

Dakalbab et al. (2024) for literature surveys focusing on deep learning and ML applications of AT.

3.3. Risk Management

Another core task in finance is risk management. In this context, *risk management* (RM) or *financial risk management* refers to the activities of firms when assessing potential risks and preventing the losses that might arise from various sources, such as the market, credits issued to customers, and the operations of the firm. The continuous identification and assessment of potential risks with a high level of accuracy is vital for firms. Among the various types of risks that a firm can face, *credit risk* defines the potential loss arising from the inability of a contracting party to fulfill its obligations (principal or interest payments on loans, etc.) or the increasing possibility of default on a transaction (loan defaults, financial distress, bankruptcy of the contracting party, etc.). *Credit risk management* (CRM) is the process of managing the firm value by identifying and preventing the losses associated with the credit risk. Thus, CRM consists of a wide spectrum of activities related to the pre-assessment of a potential contractor, post-assessment of the failure of timely payments, and default risk or bankruptcy predictions concerning a contractor.

The technological developments yielding a broad field of applications for both AI and ML are transforming the research on RM and its practices, showing potential to revolutionize RM applications in academia and the finance sector. Currently, the CRM subfield constitutes most of the academic research employing ML algorithms in RM tasks. For instance, the works by Li et al. (2004), Yu et al. (2008), Khandani et al. (2010), Lessmann et al. (2015), Luo et al. (2017), Bao et al. (2019), Ma and Lv (2019), and Emmanuel et al. (2024) focused on credit scoring, credit risk assessment, or credit risk prediction tasks. The works by Yeh and Lien (2009), Hamori et al. (2018), Moscatelli et al. (2020), Liu et al. (2022), and Bazzana et al. (2024) dealt with predictions of the default risk. Moreover, Min and Lee (2005), Min et al. (2006), Tsai (2009), Kim and Kang (2010), Wang (2017), Hosaka (2019) and Hamdi et al. (2024) considered the bankruptcy prediction problem. These works constitute only a small sample of the growing body of literature using ML algorithms in CRM tasks. The reader can also consult the works by Kumar and Ravi (2007), Chen et al. (2016), Leo et al. (2019), Kim et al. (2020), and

Montevechi et al. (2024), wherein a review on ML and RM in banks as well as in finance in general is supplied.

Another source of risk, which is termed *market risk* (MR), arises from various activities of a firm in the market, such as trading, investing, or dealing with dynamic financial markets. MR is based on risks emanating from changes in commodity prices, exchange rates, or interest rates that result in uncertainty or ambiguity in the value of the firm's assets and liabilities. The works by Groth and Muntermann (2011), Ramos-Pérez et al. (2019), Fantazzini and Zimin (2020), Al Janabi (2022), Lei and Li (2022), Arian et al. (2022), and Chen et al. (2024) are examples of research employing ML algorithms in market risk warning, forecasting, and/or assessment tasks.

Additionally, the risk inherent in the activities or operations of a firm is called *operational risk* (OR). OR refers to the direct or indirect losses arising from two types of sources. The first type is the risk emanating from the firm-specific business process, personnel, or system failures (internal events), which is termed *business risk*. The second type is the risk arising from external events that might adversely affect the operations of the firm, which is named *event risk*, such as changes in regulatory requirements, occurrence of natural disasters, various attempts at frauds, etc. (Aziz & Dowling, 2019; Mashrur et al. 2020). Among these, the event risk of fraudulent actions toward a firm's operations constitutes a significant source of OR risk. As a result, most research has discussed ML applications in *fraud detection* in a stand-alone section rather than under the heading of RM or OR management. The works by Edge and Sampaio (2009), Abbasi et al. (2012), Ahmed et al. (2016), Sadgali et al. (2018), Alghofaili et al. (2020), Shou et al. (2021), Çağlayan and Bahtiyar (2022), Alwadain et al. (2023), Marazqah Btoush et al. (2023), and Li et al. (2024) focused on detecting, estimating, or predicting financial fraud using various ML algorithms. Moreover, Ravi et al. (2009), Aquaro et al. (2010), Milkau and Bott (2018), Zhou et al. (2021), Pena et al. (2021), Pakhchanyan et al. (2022), and Chumakova et al. (2024) dealt with applications of ML in the identification, early warning, and/or prediction of OR risks in general.

3.4. FinTech

Financial technologies, which are mostly referred to as *FinTech*, are various technological developments and innovations that provide unique financial products or infrastructures and enable different financial services and applications, such as financial transactions, client services, *person-to-person (P2P) lending*, fraud detection mechanisms, financial apps, and so forth. Examples of FinTech innovations include digital currencies (Bitcoin, Litecoin, Ethereum, etc.) and blockchain technology, robo-advisors or robo-assistants, digital trading platforms, and mobile and digital payment services.

Developments in FinTech have shaped and transformed the financial industry and its services at a pace that cannot be ignored. As noted by Sanga and Aziakpono (2023), it is possible to classify the evolution of FinTech into three stages. The first stage is *FinTech 1.0*, which consists of the period from 1866 to 1967, when making fast financial transfers was made possible. The second stage, named *FinTech 2.0*, is the period 1967–2008, when various electronic payments, using ATMs and electronic settlements were made available, resulting in an improvement in traditional financial services. The last stage of *FinTech 3.0* is the period beginning in 2008 and continuing until the present. This third stage is characterized by the development of highly innovative products or services that yield an expansion or outreach of financial services, with greater financial inclusion and an improvement in schemes of alternative financing, such as insurance services using big data and mobile devices, crowdfunding, mobile money, cryptocurrencies, and digital exchange platforms.

These developments in FinTech have attracted a great deal of attention from academics, industry experts, and regulators. For instance, the works by Li et al. (2018), Chen (2018), Kim and Cho (2019), Jagtiani and Lemieux (2019), Sakarya and Aksu (2021), Ashta and Herrmann (2021), Stojanović et al. (2021), Huang et al. (2022), Özgür (2022), Rizinski et al. (2022), Mirza et al. (2023), Sharma et al. (2024), and Roy and Vasa (2024) are examples of research focusing on FinTech and ML and/or dealing with various applications of FinTech. Moreover, Sangwan et al. (2019) conducted a comprehensive review on FinTech.

3.5. Investor Behavior and Sentiment

In the finance sector, ML algorithms are also employed to model and/or predict the behaviors of financial market participants, such as investors and traders. The works by Lee and Radhakrishna (2000), Zeng et al. (2016), Silva et al. (2019), Pagliaro et al. (2021), Mavruk (2022), Kim et al. (2020), Qianyun and Xiaoyan (2021), and Nixon and Gilbert (2024) are examples of academic research using ML to model or predict various types of investor/trader behaviors.

Furthermore, a trending research topic in terms of finance empowered by the developing field of ML and AI is *sentiment analysis* (SA), which refers to the process of identifying and classifying a person's opinions as revealed in a certain text in relation to a product, service, or topic (Mishev et al. 2020). There are various methodologies employed for SA, such as ML methods, lexicon-based approaches, and hybrid approaches. SA is an essential tool for finance because investors, traders, and portfolio managers need to be able to obtain negative or positive sentiments from the news and other publicly available sources to assist in their financial analysis and decision-making processes. According to Goodell et al. (2021), SA is one of the nine foundational topics in finance that ML research is built on. Examples of the other foundational topics include valuation and asset pricing, portfolio optimization, option pricing, financial forecasting, fraud detection, and credit/financial risk.

Due to the increasing popularity of SA in finance, it is possible to identify many published papers that use SA in their research. A Google Scholar search using the keywords "sentiment analysis" and "finance" yielded 51,000 results in December 2024. Moreover, a Web of Science (all databases) search using the same keywords resulted in 1164 published works. Some examples of academic research that employs SA in various finance tasks or reviews the related literature are Das and Chen (2007), Li et al. (2009), Van de Kauter et al. (2015), Krishnamoorthy (2018), Su et al. (2021), Ameen Suhail et al. (2022), Mendi (2022), Karanikola et al. (2023), Rizinski et al. (2024), Heydarian et al. (2024), and Todd et al. (2024).

4. Applications of Machine Learning in Asset Allocation

A core area of application of the rapidly developing field of ML is portfolio asset allocation. As mentioned previously, the term asset allocation refers to a wide spectrum of activities of a financial market participant (investor, trader, etc.), including searching among various types of assets (stocks, bonds, derivatives, etc.) and their properties to construct a portfolio, considering the varying states of the world, investment periods, and individual attitudes and preferences. In this sense, different finance tasks or subfields interact with each other and contribute to the final goal of constructing a portfolio based on the predefined objectives and preferences of the investor. For instance, many of the price or excess return forecasts for financial assets discussed in the asset pricing literature are also employed to build portfolios using various portfolio allocation strategies, such as the tangency or minimum variance portfolios. The buy or sell signals of assets produced by ML algorithms in algorithmic trading practices are also used to construct portfolios, as shown in the asset pricing example. Moreover, the obtained investor sentiments are employed by different ML algorithms and portfolio allocation strategies as input variables when determining the investment proportion or weight of a given financial asset in a portfolio.

The remainder of this section will cover as many academic works as possible that use ML algorithms in portfolio selection tasks. Nevertheless, it should be kept in mind that it is not possible to exhaust all the literature on the subject and that doing so is also outside the scope of an individual chapter. As can be seen in Figure 2, ML applications in portfolio asset allocation tasks are not new. Additionally, the number of yearly publications (research and review articles) has been increasing since the 1990s. The number of articles reported in Figure 2 was obtained from the Scopus database using the keywords "portfolio selection" or "portfolio allocation" or "asset allocation" and "machine learning." However, the works reported in this chapter are restricted to articles published during the last 25 years (i.e., the period 2000–2024) and retrieved from one of the following databases: Web of Science, Scopus, or Google Scholar.

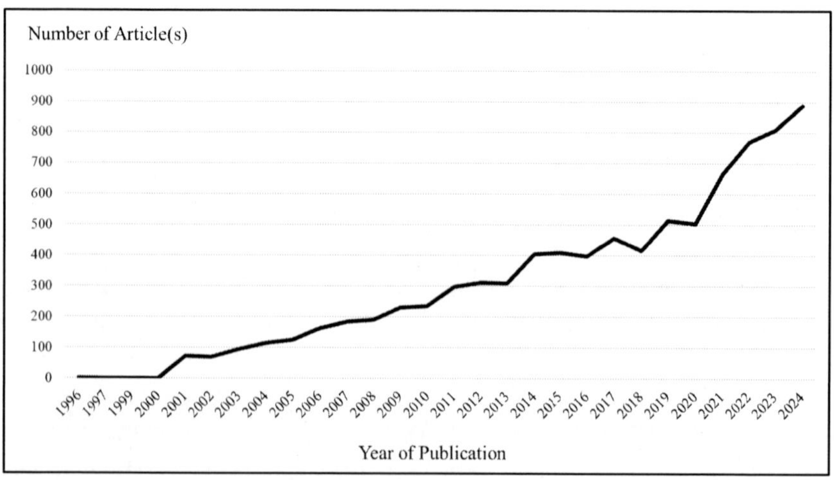

Source: Author's own illustration.

Figure 2. Publication Trend of ML in Portfolio Asset Allocation.

Table 1. Overview of Literature

Publication	Portfolio Constituents	Portfolio Asset Allocation Method	ML Algorithms
Chapados and Bengio (2001)	Complete TSE 300 index	Mean-variance (MV), neural network-based portfolio	Neural network (MLP), RNN
Lin et al. (2006)	Stocks of Taiwan stock market	RNN based portfolio, VAR	Elman RNN
Kim and Enke (2016)	KOSPI 200	Target volatility strategy	ANN
Li et al. (2016)	Stocks of HSI and NYSE, Fama–French USA 30 industry portfolio	Equally weighted portfolio (EWP), binary switch portfolio, Cover's universal portfolio, successive constant rebalanced portfolio	K-nearest neighbour (KNN)
Dehghanpour and Esfahanipour (2018)	Stocks listed on DJIA	CPPI, MV	Robust genetic programming, ANN, ANFIS
Mishra and Padhy (2019)	Stocks listed on BSE-30 and NIFTY 100	MV	Support vector regression (SVR)
Paiva et al. (2019)	Stocks of São Paulo Stock Exchange	EWP, MV	Support vector machine (SVM)
Vo et al. (2019)	Stocks listed on S&P 500	Tangency portfolio (TP), TP with ESG	BiLSTM, reinforcement learning (RL)
Wang et al. (2020)	Stocks listed on FTSE 100	MV, minimum-variance, EWP	RF, SVM, LSTM, deep neural networks (DNN)
Zhang et al. (2020)	US Indices: VTI, AGG, DBC, VIX	TP, EWP, fixed allocation, maximum diversification, diversity weighted portfolio, deep learning (DL) based portfolio	LSTM
Chen et al. (2021)	Stocks listed on SSE 50	TP, EWP	XGBoost, LSTM, SVR, Hybrid of XGBoost and firefly algorithm
Jaeger et al. (2021)	Futures	Inverse variance, ERC, HRP, Naive RP	XGBoost

Table 1. (continued)

Publication	Portfolio Constituents	Portfolio Asset Allocation Method	ML Algorithms
Kwak et al. (2021)	Stocks listed on S&P 500	EWP, DNN based portfolio	Deep neural network (DNN)
Ma et al. (2021)	Stocks listed on CSI 100	Mean-variance (MV), Omega portfolio	RF, SVR, LSTM, CNN, deep multilayer perceptron (DMLP)
Min et al. (2021)	Fama–French USA 30 industry portfolio	MV, Black-Litterman, EWP, worst-case robust portfolio	Logistic regression, SVR, RF, XGBoost, MLP (ANN)
Papenbrock et al. (2021)	Futures	HRP, ERC	Multiobjective evolutionary algorithm
Zhang and Chen (2021)	Stocks on Choice Database	Extended GMV and TP portfolios including ESG performance	Hybrid of genetic algorithm and ELM (extreme learning machine)
Chaweewanchon and Chaysiri (2022)	Stocks listed on SET 50	MV, EWP	CNN, LSTM, BiLSTM, hybrid of CNN and BiLSTM
Chen et al. (2022)	Stocks listed on CSI 100	Modified mean–variance	RF, LSTM, SVR, ELM, ANN
Du (2022)	Stocks listed on CSI 300 and S&P 500	EWP, MV	RF, SVM, attention-based LSTM
Kaczmarek and Perez (2022)	Stocks listed on S&P 500 and STOXX 600	TP, EWP, hierarchical risk parity (HRP)	Random forest (RF)
Cui et al. (2023)	Cryptocurrencies	MV, mean-CVaR	Deep reinforcement learning (DRL)
Caparrini et al. (2024)	Stocks listed on S&P 500	EWP	RF, decision tree, XGBoost
Cortés et al. (2024)	Stocks	EWP, MV, RL based portfolios	LSTM, reinforcement learning (RL)
Jiang et al. (2024)	Stocks listed on DJIA and S&P 100	MV, TP, DRL based portfolios	DRL

An early work on the subject was the research by Chapados and Bengio (2001), who proposed an asset allocation method that controls the value-at-risk (VaR) of a portfolio using the neural network (NN) algorithm. The researchers employed a data set consisting of 14 subindices of the TSE 300 (Toronto Stock Exchange) index for the period January 1971–July 1996. Each subindex represents a sector of the Canadian economy. According to the estimated performance metrics, Chapados and Bengio (2001) argued that the proposed NN method with a VaR-adjusted criteria was successful. Moreover, the obtained results were comparable to a traditional forecasting method employed in conjunction with the mean-variance (MV) portfolio allocation.

Almahdi and Yang (2017) used the recurrent reinforcement learning algorithm (RRL) to construct an optimal portfolio based on the expected maximum drawdown risk measure, particularly the Calmar ratio. The authors used five exchange-traded funds (iShares Russell 1000, iShares Micro-Cap, SPDR S&P 500, Wisdom Tree Emerging Markets High Dividend, iShares Credit Bond) as the portfolio constituents for the period from January 1, 2011 to December 31, 2015. Almahdi and Yang (2017) compared the portfolio allocation performance of the RRL depending on (or with an objective function of) the Sharpe ratio, Calmar ratio, or Sterling ratio. As a result, three portfolios were formed and named the SR-RRL for the Sharpe ratio-, TR-RRL for the Sterling ratio-, and CR-RRL for the Calmar ratio-dependent portfolios. Overall, the results indicated the outperformance of the RRL portfolios using the Calmar ratio when compared with the others employed in the research.

Koratamaddi et al. (2021) employed a unique deep reinforcement learning (DRL) algorithm that uses the overall opinion or attitude of investors toward a financial asset or market called the *market segment* and the historical price data in a portfolio selection task. To test the unique DRL approach, the researchers employed 30 stocks that were listed in the Dow Jones Industrial Average (DJIA) index during the period January 1, 2001 to October 2, 2018. Koratamaddi et al. (2021) selected four portfolio performance measures—namely, the Sharpe ratio, annualized return, standard deviation, and terminal portfolio value—to compare different allocation methods, such as the mean-variance portfolios. In terms of the estimated portfolio performance metrics, Koratamaddi et al. (2021) argued that the proposed method yielded better results than the others employed in the research.

In a more recent work, Owen (2023) used hierarchical clustering to improve estimates of the conditional covariance in a portfolio optimization task. The researcher employed the monthly returns of stocks listed on three stock exchanges—namely, the AMEX, NYSE, and NASDAQ—for the period from 1965 to 2017. Owen (2023) considered three look-back periods in the estimation of the covariance matrix: 12, 60 and 120 months. The researcher compared the cluster-optimized long-only portfolios to the market portfolio and the mean-variance portfolio of Markowitz (1952) for a three-month holding period. The results indicated an improvement in the portfolio performance relative to the other benchmarks when hierarchical clustering was used to construct the portfolios.

Table 1 gives a comprehensive overview of the literature. Additionally, the reader can consult the works by Metaxiotis and Liagkouras (2012), Snow (2020a), Snow (2020b), Bartram et al. (2021), Asawa (2022), Novykov et al. (2023), and López de Prado et al. (2024), wherein either the topic of ML in portfolio construction is extensively explained or a review of the literature focusing on ML applications in portfolio asset allocation tasks is provided.

5. Challenges and Future Prospects

While the field of ML has attracted well-deserved attention from scholars and finance experts, there remain several challenges during the implementation of ML applications in the finance sector. Among the most important of these challenges is the quality and characteristics of financial data. More specifically, financial data sets are highly dynamic and complex, typically including noise, missing values, and inconsistencies. Moreover, non-stationary and highly volatile financial data can easily lead to the *overfitting* problem of ML algorithms. While an overfitted algorithm exhibits good performance in relation to the training sample, it does not perform as well as on unseen, out-of-sample data.

The other challenges when applying ML are related to the single-tasking property of modern ML methods and the need to develop new methods depending on the task, model features, interpretability of the employed algorithms, privacy and ethical concerns, biases stemming from the employed data or forecasts of analysts, and regulatory concerns (Mukhamediev et al. 2022; Mienye et al. 2024; Ajiga et al. 2024).

Nevertheless, the importance of the field of ML and its further potential for applications in the finance sector are undeniable. Indeed, it can safely be said that there are significant opportunities and prospects in terms of applying ML in finance, both in academic research and in industry applications. For instance, the accuracy of various forecasting tasks (asset prices, returns and volatility, etc.) might be improved through the development of new ML methods, while the data quality and availability might be increased by using AI-driven autonomous technology in financial transactions, services, etc. Moreover, as the field of ML develops, it will create its own path toward new applications and research opportunities by overcoming or removing the challenges discussed in this section.

References

Abbasi, A., Albrecht, C., Vance, A., & Hansen, J. (2012). MetaFraud: A Meta-Learning Framework for Detecting Financial Fraud. *MIS Quarterly*, *36*(4), 1293–1327. https://doi.org/10.2307/41703508.

Ahmed, M., Mahmood, A. N., & Islam, M. R. (2016). A Survey of Anomaly Detection Techniques in Financial Domain. *Future Generation Computer Systems*, *55*, 278–288. https://doi.org/10.1016/j.future.2015.01.001.

Ajiga, D. I., Adeleye, R. A., Tubokirifuruar, T. S., Bello, B. G., Ndubuisi, N. L., Asuzu, O. F., & Owolabi, O. R. (2024). Machine Learning for Stock Market Forecasting: A Review of Models and Accuracy. *Finance & Accounting Research Journal*, *6*(2), 112–124. https://doi.org/10.51594/farj.v6i2.783.

Al Janabi, M. A. M. (2022). Optimization Algorithms and Investment Portfolio Analytics with Machine Learning Techniques Under Time-Varying Liquidity Constraints. *Journal of Modelling in Management*, *17*(3), 864–895. https://doi.org/10.1108/JM2-10-2020-0259.

Alghofaili, Y., Albattah, A., & Rassam, M. A. (2020). A Financial Fraud Detection Model Based on LSTM Deep Learning Technique. *Journal of Applied Security Research*, *15*(4), 498–516. https://doi.org/10.1080/19361610.2020.1815491.

Almahdi, S., & Yang, S. Y. (2017). An Adaptive Portfolio Trading System: A Risk-Return Portfolio Optimization Using Recurrent Reinforcement Learning with Expected Maximum Drawdown. *Expert Systems with Applications*, *87*, 267–279. https://doi.org/10.1016/j.eswa.2017.06.023.

Alwadain A., Ali, R. F., & Muneer, A. (2023). Estimating Financial Fraud through Transaction-Level Features and Machine Learning. *Mathematics*, *11*(5), 1184. https://doi.org/10.3390/math11051184.

Ameen Suhail, K. M., Sankar, S., Kumar, A. S., Nestor, T., Soliman, N. F., Algarni, A. D., El-Shafai, W., & Abd El-Samie, F. E. (2022). Stock Market Trading Based on Market Sentiments and Reinforcement Learning. *Computers, Materials & Continua*, *70*(1), 935–950. https://doi.org/10.32604/cmc.2022.017069.

Aquaro, V., Bardoscia, M., Bellotti, R., Consiglio, A., De Carlo, F., & Ferri, G. (2010). A Bayesian Networks Approach to Operational Risk. *Physica A: Statistical Mechanics and its Applications*, *389*(8), 1721–1728. https://doi.org/10.1016/j.physa.2009.12.043.

Arian, H., Moghimi, M., Tabatabaei, E., & Zamani, S. (2022). Encoded Value-at-Risk: A Machine Learning Approach for Portfolio Risk Measurement. *Mathematics and*

Computers in Simulation, *202*, 500–525. https://doi.org/10.1016/j.matcom.2022.07.015.

Asawa, Y. S. (2022). Modern Machine Learning Solutions for Portfolio Selection. *IEEE Engineering Management Review*, *50*(1), 94–112. https://doi.org/10.1109/EMR.2021.3131158.

Ashta, A., & Herrmann, H. (2021). Artificial Intelligence and Fintech: An Overview of Opportunities and Risks for Banking, Investments, and Microfinance. *Strategic Change*, *30*(3), 211–222. https://doi.org/10.1002/jsc.2404.

Aziz, S., & Dowling, M. (2019). Machine Learning and AI for Risk Management. In T. Lynn, J. Mooney, P. Rosati, & M. Cummins (Eds.) *Disrupting Finance* (pp. 33–50). Palgrave Studies in Digital Business & Enabling Technologies, Palgrave Pivot, Cham. https://doi.org/10.1007/978-3-030-02330-0_3.

Bao, W., Lianju, N., & Yue, K. (2019). Integration of Unsupervised and Supervised Machine Learning Algorithms for Credit Risk Assessment. *Expert Systems with Applications*, *128*, 301–315. https://doi.org/10.1016/j.eswa.2019.02.033.

Bartram, S. M., Branke, J., De Rossi, G., & Motahari, M. (2021) Machine Learning for Active Portfolio Management. *Journal of Financial Data Science*, *3*(3), 9–30. https://doi.org/10.3905/jfds.2021.1.071.

Bazzana, F., Bee, M., & Hussin Adam Khatir, A. A. (2024). Machine Learning Techniques for Default Prediction: An Application to Small Italian Companies. *Risk Management*, *26*, 1. https://doi.org/10.1057/s41283-023-00132-2.

Bianchi, D., Büchner, M., & Tamoni, A. (2021). Bond Risk Premiums with Machine Learning. *The Review of Financial Studies*, *34*(2), 1046–1089. https://doi.org/10.1093/rfs/hhaa062.

Bishop, C. M. (1995). *Neural Networks for Pattern Recognition*. Oxford University Press.

Caparrini, A., Arroyo, J., & Mansilla, J. E. (2024). S&P 500 Stock Selection Using Machine Learning Classifiers: A Look into the Changing Role of Factors. *Research in International Business and Finance*, *70*, 102336. https://doi.org/10.1016/j.ribaf.2024.102336.

Carbonell, J. G., Michalski, R. S., & Mitchell, T. M. (1983). 1 - An Overview of Machine Learning. In R. S. Michalski, J. G. Carbonell, & T. M. Mitchell (Eds.) *Machine Learning* (pp. 3–23). Morgan Kaufmann. https://doi.org/10.1016/B978-0-08-051054-5.50005-4.

Chapados, N., & Bengio, Y. (2001). Cost Functions and Model Combination for VaR-Based Asset Allocation Using Neural Networks. *IEEE Transactions on Neural Networks*, *12*(4), 890–906. https://doi.org/10.1109/72.935098.

Chaweewanchon, A., & Chaysiri, R. (2022). Markowitz Mean-Variance Portfolio Optimization with Predictive Stock Selection Using Machine Learning. *International Journal of Financial Studies*, *10*(3), 64. https://doi.org/10.3390/ijfs10030064.

Chen, K. (2018). Financial Innovation and Technology Firms: A Smart New World with Machines. *Banking and Finance Issues in Emerging Markets, International Symposia in Economic Theory and Econometrics* (Vol. 25, pp. 279–292). Emerald Publishing Limited. https://doi.org/10.1108/S1571-038620180000025012.

Chen, N., Ribeiro, B., & Chen, A. (2016). Financial Credit Risk Assessment: A Recent Review. *Artificial Intelligence Review*, *45*, 1–23. https://doi.org/10.1007/s10462-015-9434-x.

Chen, W., Chen, B., & Cai, X. (2024). Forecasting China's Stock Market Risk Under the Background of the Stock Connect Programs. *Soft Computing*, *28*, 2483–2499. https://doi.org/10.1007/s00500-023-08496-z.

Chen, W., Zhang, H., & Jia, L. (2022). A Novel Two-Stage Method for Well-Diversified Portfolio Construction Based on Stock Return Prediction Using Machine Learning. *The North American Journal of Economics and Finance*, *63*, 101818. https://doi.org/10.1016/j.najef.2022.101818.

Chen, W., Zhang, H., Mehlawat, M. K., & Jia, L. (2021). Mean–Variance Portfolio Optimization Using Machine Learning-Based Stock Price Prediction. *Applied Soft Computing*, *100*, 106943. https://doi.org/10.1016/j.asoc.2020.106943.

Chumakova, E. V., Korneev, D. G., Gasparian, M. S., & Makhov, I. S. (2024). Application of Neural Network Technologies to Assess the Competence of Personnel in the tasks of Controlling the Operational Risk of a Credit Institution. *Business Informatics*, *18*(2), 7–21. https://doi.org/10.17323/2587-814X.2024.2.7.21.

Cortes, C., & Vapnik, V. (1995). Support-Vector Networks. *Machine Learning*, *20*(3), 273–297.

Cortés, D. G., Onieva, E., Pastor, I., Trinchera, L., & Wu, J. (2024). Portfolio Construction Using Explainable Reinforcement Learning. *Expert Systems*, *41*(11), e13667. https://doi.org/10.1111/exsy.13667.

Cui, T., Ding, S., Jin, H., & Zhang, Y. (2023). Portfolio Constructions in Cryptocurrency Market: A CVaR-Based Deep Reinforcement Learning Approach. *Economic Modelling*, *119*, 106078. https://doi.org/10.1016/j.econmod.2022.106078.

Culkin, R., & Das, S. (2017) Machine Learning in Finance: The Case of Deep Learning for Option Pricing. *Working Paper*, Santa Clara University.

Çağlayan, M., & Bahtiyar, Ş. (2022). Money Laundering Detection with Node2Vec. *Gazi University Journal of Science*, *35*(3), 854–873. https://doi.org/10.35378/gujs.854725.

Çelik, Ö., & Altunaydın, S. S. (2018). A Research on Machine Learning Methods and Its Applications. *Journal of Educational Technology & Online Learning*, *1*(3), 25–40. https://doi.org/10.31681\jetol.457046.

Dakalbab, F., Talib, M. A., Nasir, Q., & Saroufil, T. (2024). Artificial Intelligence Techniques in Financial Trading: A Systematic Literature Review. *Journal of King Saud University - Computer and Information Sciences*, *36*, 102015. https://doi.org/10.1016/j.jksuci.2024.102015.

Das, S. R., & Chen, M. Y. (2007). Yahoo! for Amazon: Sentiment Extraction from Small Talk on the Web. *Management Science*, *53*(9), 1375–1388. https://doi.org/10.1287/mnsc.1070.0704.

Dehghanpour, S., & Esfahanipour, A. (2018) Dynamic Portfolio Insurance Strategy: A Robust Machine Learning Approach, *Journal of Information and Telecommunication*, *2*(4), 392–410. https://doi.org/10.1080/24751839.2018.1431447.

Dixon, M. F., Halperin, I., & Bilokon, P. (2020). *Machine Learning in Finance: From Theory to Practice*. Springer Nature Switzerland, AG. https://doi.org/10.1007/978-3-030-41068-1.

Du, J. (2022). Mean–Variance Portfolio Optimization with Deep Learning Based-Forecasts for Cointegrated Stocks. *Expert Systems with Applications*, *201*, 117005. https://doi.org/10.1016/j.eswa.2022.117005.

Edge, M. E., & Sampaio, P. R. F. (2009). A Survey of Signature Based Methods for Financial Fraud Detection. *Computers & Security*, *28*(6), 381–394. https://doi.org/10.1016/j.cose.2009.02.001.

El Naqa, I., & Murphy, M. J. (2015). What Is Machine Learning? In I. El Naqa, R. Li, & M. Murphy (Eds.) *Machine Learning in Radiation Oncology*. Springer, Cham. https://doi.org/10.1007/978-3-319-18305-3_1.

Emmanuel, I., Sun, Y., & Wang, Z. (2024). A Machine Learning-Based Credit Risk Prediction Engine System Using a Stacked Classifier and a Filter-Based Feature Selection Method. *Journal of Big Data*, *11*(1), 23. https://doi.org/10.1186/s40537-024-00882-0.

Emmert-Streib, F., Moutari, S., & Dehmer, M. (2023). *Elements of Data Science, Machine Learning, and Artificial Intelligence Using R*. Springer. https://doi.org/10.1007/978-3-031-13339-8.

Fallahgoul, H., Franstianto, V., & Lin, X. (2024). Asset Pricing with Neural Networks: Significance Tests. *Journal of Econometrics*, *238*, 105574. https://doi.org/10.1016/j.jeconom.2023.105574.

Fantazzini, D., & Zimin, S. (2020). A Multivariate Approach for the Simultaneous Modelling of Market Risk and Credit Risk for Cryptocurrencies. *Journal of Industrial and Business Economics*, *47*, 19–69. https://doi.org/10.1007/s40812-019-00136-8.

Fix, E., Hodges, J. L. (1989). Discriminatory Analysis. Nonparametric Discrimination: Consistency Properties. *International Statistical Review*, *57*(3), 238–247. https://doi.org/10.2307/1403797.

Giglio, S., Kelly, B., & Xiu, D. (2022). Factor Models, Machine Learning, and Asset Pricing. *Annual Review of Financial Economics*, *14*(1), 337–368. https://doi.org/10.1146/annurev-financial-101521-104735.

Grant, T. D., & Wischik, D. J. (2020). *On the Path to AI*. Palgrave Macmillan, Cham. https://doi.org/10.1007/978-3-030-43582-0.

Groth, S. S., & Muntermann, J. (2011). An Intraday Market Risk Management Approach Based on Textual Analysis. *Decision Support Systems*, *50*(4), 680–691. https://doi.org/10.1016/j.dss.2010.08.019.

Gu, S., Kelly, B., & Xiu, D. (2020). Empirical Asset Pricing via Machine Learning. *The Review of Financial Studies*, *33*(5), 2223–2273. https://doi.org/10.1093/rfs/hhaa009.

Gu, S., Kelly, B., & Xiu, D. (2021). Autoencoder Asset Pricing Models. *Journal of Econometrics*, *222*(1), 429–450. https://doi.org/10.1016/j.jeconom.2020.07.009.

Gupta, R., Srivastava, D., Sahu, M., Tiwari, S., Ambasta, R. K., & Kumar, P. (2021). Artificial Intelligence to Deep Learning: Machine Intelligence Approach for Drug Discovery. *Molecular Diversity*, *25*, 1315–1360. https://doi.org/10.1007/s11030-021-10217-3.

Habbab, F. Z., & Kampouridis, M. (2024). An In-depth Investigation of Five Machine Learning Algorithms for Optimizing Mixed-Asset Portfolios Including REITs. *Expert Systems with Applications*, *235*, 121102. https://doi.org/10.1016/j.eswa.2023.121102.

Hady, M. F. A., & Schwenker, F. (2013). Semi-Supervised Learning. In M. Bianchini, M. Maggini, & L. Jain (Eds.) *Handbook on Neural Information Processing. Intelligent Systems Reference Library* (Vol. 49, pp. 215–239). Springer. https://doi.org/10.1007/978-3-642-36657-4_7.

Hamdi, M., Mestiri, S., & Arbi, A. (2024). Artificial Intelligence Techniques for Bankruptcy Prediction of Tunisian Companies: An Application of Machine Learning and Deep Learning-Based Models. *Journal of Risk and Financial Management*, *17*, 132. https://doi.org/10.3390/jrfm17040132.

Hamori, S., Kawai, M., Kume, T., Murakami, Y., & Watanabe, C. (2018). Ensemble Learning or Deep Learning? Application to Default Risk Analysis. *Journal of Risk and Financial Management*, *11*(1), 12. https://doi.org/10.3390/jrfm11010012.

Hastie, T., Tibshirani, R., & Friedman, J. (2009). *The Elements of Statistical Learning: Data Mining, Inference, and Prediction* (2nd ed.). Springer Series in Statistics, Springer. https://doi.org/10.1007/978-0-387-84858-7.

Heydarian, P., Bifet, A., & Corbet, S. (2024). Understanding Market Sentiment Analysis: A Survey. *Journal of Economic Surveys*, 1–23. https://doi.org/10.1111/joes.12645.

Hosaka, T. (2019). Bankruptcy Prediction Using Imaged Financial Ratios and Convolutional Neural Networks. *Expert Systems with Applications*, *117*, 287–299. https://doi.org/10.1016/j.eswa.2018.09.039.

Hu, Y., Liu, K., Zhang, X., Su, L., Ngai, E. W. T., & Liu, M. (2015). Application of Evolutionary Computation for Rule Discovery in Stock Algorithmic Trading: A Literature Review. *Applied Soft Computing*, *36*, 534–551. https://doi.org/10.1016/j.asoc.2015.07.008.

Huang, S. C., Wu, C. F., Chiou, C. C., & Lin, M. C. (2022). Intelligent FinTech Data Mining by Advanced Deep Learning Approaches. *Computational Economics*, *59*, 1407–1422. https://doi.org/10.1007/s10614-021-10118-5.

Jaeger, M., Krügel, S., Marinelli, D., Papenbrock, J., & Schwendner, P. (2021). Interpretable Machine Learning for Diversified Portfolio Construction. *The Journal of Financial Data Science*, *3*(3), 31–51.

Jagtiani J., & Lemieux, C. (2019). The Roles of Alternative Data and Machine Learning in Fintech Lending: Evidence from the LendingClub Consumer Platform. *Financial Management*, *48*, 1009–1029. https://doi.org/10.1111/fima.12295.

Jiang, Y., Olmo, J., & Atwi, M. (2024). Deep Reinforcement Learning for Portfolio Selection. *Global Finance Journal*, *62*, 101016. https://doi.org/10.1016/j.gfj.2024.101016.

Joshi, A. V. (2023). *Machine Learning and Artificial Intelligence* (2nd ed.). Springer Nature Switzerland AG. https://doi.org/10.1007/978-3-031-12282-8.

Kaczmarek, T., & Perez, K. (2022) Building Portfolios Based on Machine Learning Predictions. *Economic Research-Ekonomska Istraživanja*, *35*(1), 19–37. https://doi.org/10.1080/1331677X.2021.1875865.

Karanikola, A., Davrazos, G., Liapis, C. M., & Kotsiantis, S. (2023). Financial Sentiment Analysis: Classic Methods vs. Deep Learning Models. *Intelligent Decision Technologies*, *17*(4), 893–915. https://doi.org/10.3233/IDT-230478.

Khan, N., & Hassan, A. (2024). Do Decimated Based Trading Model Outperform the Buy-and-Hold Investment Strategy. *Economic Computation and Economic Cybernetics Studies & Research*, *58*(1), 229–243. https://doi.org/10.24818/18423264/58.1.24.15.

Khandani, A. E., Kim, A. J., & Lo, A. W. (2010). Consumer Credit-Risk models via Machine-Learning Algorithms. *Journal of Banking & Finance*, *34*(11), 2767–2787. https://doi.org/10.1016/j.jbankfin.2010.06.001.

Kim, A., Yang, Y., Lessmann, S., Ma, T., Sung, M. C., & Johnson, J. E. (2020). Can Deep Learning Predict Risky Retail Investors? A Case Study in Financial Risk Behavior Forecasting. *European Journal of Operational Research*, *283*(1), 217–234. https://doi.org/10.1016/j.ejor.2019.11.007.

Kim, J.-Y., & Cho, S.-B. (2019). Towards Repayment Prediction in Peer-to-Peer Social Lending Using Deep Learning. *Mathematics*, *7*(11), 1041. https://doi.org/10.3390/math7111041.

Kim, H., Cho, H., & Ryu, D. (2020). Corporate Default Predictions Using Machine Learning: Literature Review. *Sustainability*, *12*, 6325. https://doi.org/10.3390/su12166325.

Kim, M. J., & Kang, D. K. (2010). Ensemble with Neural Networks for Bankruptcy Prediction. *Expert Systems with Applications*, *37*(4), 3373–3379. https://doi.org/10.1016/j.eswa.2009.10.012.

Kim, Y., & Enke, D. (2016). Using Neural Networks to Forecast Volatility for an Asset Allocation Strategy Based on the Target Volatility. *Procedia Computer Science*, *95*, 281–286. https://doi.org/10.1016/j.procs.2016.09.335.

Koratamaddi, P., Wadhwani, K., Gupta, M., & Sanjeevi, S. G. (2021). Market Sentiment-Aware Deep Reinforcement Learning Approach for Stock Portfolio Allocation. *Engineering Science and Technology, an International Journal*, *24*(4), 848–859. https://doi.org/10.1016/j.jestch.2021.01.007.

Krishnamoorthy, S. (2018). Sentiment Analysis of Financial News Articles Using Performance Indicators. *Knowledge and Information Systems*, *56*(2), 373–394. https://doi.org/10.1007/s10115-017-1134-1.

Kumar, P. R., & Ravi, V. (2007). Bankruptcy Prediction in Banks and Firms via Statistical and Intelligent Techniques – A Review. *European Journal of Operational Research*, *180*(1), 1–28. https://doi.org/10.1016/j.ejor.2006.08.043.

Kwak, Y., Song, J., & Lee, H. (2021). Neural Network with Fixed Noise for Index-Tracking Portfolio Optimization. *Expert Systems with Applications*, *183*, 115298. https://doi.org/10.1016/j.eswa.2021.115298.

Lee, C. M., & Radhakrishna, B. (2000). Inferring Investor Behavior: Evidence from TORQ Data. *Journal of Financial Markets*, *3*(2), 83–111.

Lei, Y., & Li, Y. (2022). Construction and Simulation of the Market Risk Early-Warning Model Based on Deep Learning Methods. *Scientific Programming*, 4733220. https://doi.org/10.1155/2022/4733220.

Leo, M., Sharma, S., & Maddulety, K. (2019). Machine Learning in Banking Risk Management: A Literature Review. *Risks*, *7*(1), 29. https://doi.org/10.3390/risks7010029.

Lessmann, S., Baesens, B., Seow, H. & Thomas, L. C., (2015). Benchmarking State-of-the-Art Classification Algorithms for Credit Scoring: An Update of Research. *European*

Journal of Operational Research, *247*(1), 124–136. https://doi.org/10.1016/j.ejor.2015.05.030.

Li, J., Liu, J., Xu, W., & Shi, Y. (2004). Support Vector Machines Approach to Credit Assessment. In M. Bubak, G. D. van Albada, P. M. A. Sloot, & J. Dongarra (Eds.) *Computational Science - ICCS 2004. ICCS 2004. Lecture Notes in Computer Science* (Vol. 3039). Springer. https://doi.org/10.1007/978-3-540-25944-2_115.

Li, J., Guo, C., Lv, S., Xie, Q., & Zheng, X. (2024). Financial Fraud Detection for Chinese Listed Firms: Does Managers' Abnormal Tone Matter? *Emerging Markets Review*, *62*, 101170. https://doi.org/10.1016/j.ememar.2024.101170.

Li, N., Liang, X., Li, X., Wang, C., & Wu, D. D. (2009). Network Environment and Financial Risk Using Machine Learning and Sentiment Analysis. *Human and Ecological Risk Assessment*, *15*(2), 227–252.

Li, T., Chen, K., Feng, Y., & Ying, Z. (2016). Binary Switch Portfolio. *Quantitative Finance*, *17*(5), 763–780. https://doi.org/10.1080/14697688.2016.1223337.

Li, Z., Wu, L., & Tang, H. (2018). Optimizing the Borrowing Limit and Interest Rate in P2P System: From Borrowers' Perspective. *Scientific Programming*, 2613739. https://doi.org/10.1155/2018/2613739.

Lin, C. M., Huang, J. J., Gen, M., & Tzeng, G. H. (2006). Recurrent Neural Network for Dynamic Portfolio Selection. *Applied Mathematics and Computation*, *175*(2), 1139–1146. https://doi.org/10.1016/j.amc.2005.08.031.

Liu, Y., Yang, M., Wang, Y., Li, Y., Xiong, T., & Li, A. (2022). Applying Machine Learning Algorithms to Predict Default Probability in the Online Credit Market: Evidence from China. *International Review of Financial Analysis*, *79*, 101971. https://doi.org/10.1016/j.irfa.2021.101971.

López de Prado, M., Simonian, J., Fabozzi, F. A., & Fabozzi, F. J. (2024). Enhancing Markowitz's Portfolio Selection Paradigm with Machine Learning. *Annals of Operations Research*, 1–22. https://doi.org/10.1007/s10479-024-06257-1.

Luo, C., Wu, D., & Wu, D. (2017). A Deep Learning Approach for Credit Scoring Using Credit Default Swaps. *Engineering Applications of Artificial Intelligence*, *65*, 465–470. https://doi.org/10.1016/j.engappai.2016.12.002.

Ma, X., & Lv, S. (2019). Financial Credit Risk Prediction in Internet Finance Driven by Machine Learning. *Neural Computing and Applications*, *31*(12), 8359–8367. https://doi.org/10.1007/s00521-018-3963-6.

Ma, Y., Han, R., & Wang, W. (2021). Portfolio Optimization with Return Prediction Using Deep Learning and Machine Learning. *Expert Systems with Applications*, *165*, 113973. https://doi.org/10.1016/j.eswa.2020.113973.

Manyika, J. (2022). Getting AI Right: Introductory Notes on AI & Society. *Dædalus*, *151*(2), 5–27. https://doi.org/10.1162/daed_e_01897.

Marazqah Btoush E. A. L., Zhou, X., Gururajan, R., Chan, K. C., Genrich, R., & Sankaran, P. (2023). A Systematic Review of Literature on Credit Card Cyber Fraud Detection Using Machine and Deep Learning. *PeerJ Computer Science*, 9:e1278. https://doi.org/10.7717/peerj-cs.1278.

Markowitz, H. (1952). Portfolio Selection. *Journal of Finance*, *7*(1), 77–91.

Mashrur, A., Luo, W., Zaidi, N. A., & Robles-Kelly, A. (2020). Machine Learning for Financial Risk Management: A Survey. *IEEE Access*, *8*, 203203–203223. https://doi.org/10.1109/ACCESS.2020.3036322.

Mavruk, T. (2022). Analysis of Herding Behavior in Individual Investor Portfolios Using Machine Learning Algorithms. *Research in International Business and Finance*, *62*, 101740. https://doi.org/10.1016/j.ribaf.2022.101740.

McCarthy, J., Minsky, M., Rochester, N., & Shannon, C. (1955). A Proposal for the Dartmouth Summer Research Project on Artificial Intelligence. http://raysolomonoff.com/dartmouth/boxa/dart564props.pdf.

McCulloch, W. S., Pitts, W. (1943). A Logical Calculus of the Ideas Immanent in Nervous Activity. *The Bulletin of Mathematical Biophysics*, *5*(4), 115–133. https://doi.org/10.1007/BF02478259.

Mendi, A. F. (2022). A Sentiment Analysis Method Based on a Blockchain-Supported Long Short-Term Memory Deep Network. *Sensors*, *22*, 4419. https://doi.org/10.3390/s22124419.

Metaxiotis, K., & Liagkouras, K. (2012). Multiobjective Evolutionary Algorithms for Portfolio Management: A Comprehensive Literature Review. *Expert Systems with Applications*, *39*(14), 11685–11698. https://doi.org/10.1016/j.eswa.2012.04.053.

Mienye, E., Jere, N., Obaido, G., Mienye, I. D., & Aruleba, K. (2024). Deep Learning in Finance: A Survey of Applications and Techniques. *AI*, *5*, 2066–2091. https://doi.org/10.3390/ai5040101.

Milkau, U., & Bott, J. (2018). Active Management of Operational Risk in the Regimes of the "Unknown": What Can Machine Learning or Heuristics Deliver? *Risks*, *6*(2), 41. https://doi.org/10.3390/risks6020041.

Min, J. H., & Lee, Y. -C. (2005). Bankruptcy Prediction Using Support Vector Machine with Optimal Choice of Kernel Function Parameters. *Expert Systems with Applications*, *28*(4), 603–614. https://doi.org/10.1016/j.eswa.2004.12.008.

Min, L., Dong, J., Liu, D., & Kong, X. (2021). A Black-Litterman Portfolio Selection Model with Investor Opinions Generating from Machine Learning Algorithms. *Engineering Letters*, *29*(2), 710–721.

Min, S. H., Lee, J., & Han, I. (2006). Hybrid Genetic Algorithms and Support Vector Machines for Bankruptcy Prediction. *Expert Systems with Applications*, *31*(3), 652–660. https://doi.org/10.1016/j.eswa.2005.09.070.

Mirza, N., Elhoseny, M., Umar, M., & Metawa, N. (2023). Safeguarding FinTech Innovations with Machine Learning: Comparative Assessment of Various Approaches. *Research in International Business and Finance*, *66*, 102009. https://doi.org/10.1016/j.ribaf.2023.102009.

Mishev, K., Gjorgjevikj, A., Vodenska, I., Chitkushev, L. T., & Trajanov, D. (2020). Evaluation of Sentiment Analysis in Finance: From Lexicons to Transformers. *IEEE Access*, *8*, 131662–131682. https://doi.org/10.1109/ACCESS.2020.3009626.

Mishra, S., & Padhy, S. (2019). An Efficient Portfolio Construction Model Using Stock Price Predicted by Support Vector Regression. *The North American Journal of Economics and Finance*, *50*, 101027. https://doi.org/10.1016/j.najef.2019.101027.

Mitchell, T. M. (1997). Does Machine Learning Really Work? *AI Magazine*, *18*(3), 11–20.

Montevechi, A. A., de Carvalho Miranda, R., Medeiros, A. L., & Montevechi, J. A. B. (2024). Advancing Credit Risk Modelling with Machine Learning: A Comprehensive Review of the State-of-the-Art. *Engineering Applications of Artificial Intelligence*, *137*, 109082. https://doi.org/10.1016/j.engappai.2024.109082.

Moscatelli, M., Parlapiano, F., Narizzano, S., & Viggiano, G. (2020). Corporate Default Forecasting with Machine Learning. *Expert Systems with Applications*, *161*, 113567. https://doi.org/10.1016/j.eswa.2020.113567.

Mukhamediev, R. I., Popova, Y., Kuchin, Y., Zaitseva, E., Kalimoldayev, A., Symagulov, A., Levashenko, V., Abdoldina, F., Gopejenko, V., Yakunin, K., Muhamedijeva, E, & Yelis, M. (2022). Review of Artificial Intelligence and Machine Learning Technologies: Classification, Restrictions, Opportunities and Challenges. *Mathematics*, *10*(15), 2552. https://doi.org/10.3390/math10152552.

Nagel, S. (2021). *Machine Learning in Asset Pricing*. Princeton University Press.

Nixon, P., & Gilbert, E. (2024). Using Machine Learning to Predict Investors' Switching Behaviour. *Journal of Behavioral and Experimental Finance*, *44*, 100992. https://doi.org/10.1016/j.jbef.2024.100992.

Novykov, V., Bilson, C., Gepp, A., Harris, G., & Vanstone, B. J. (2023). Deep Learning Applications in Investment Portfolio Management: A Systematic Literature Review. *Journal of Accounting Literature*. https://doi.org/10.1108/JAL-07-2023-0119.

Olorunnimbe, K., & Viktor, H. (2023). Deep Learning in the Stock Market — a Systematic Survey of Practice, Backtesting, and Applications. *Artificial Intelligence Review*, *56*, 2057–2109. https://doi.org/10.1007/s10462-022-10226-0.

Ozbayoglu, A. M., Gudelek, M. U., & Sezer, O. B. (2020). Deep Learning for Financial Applications: A Survey. *Applied Soft Computing Journal*, *93*, 106384. https://doi.org/10.1016/j.asoc.2020.106384.

Özgür, C., & Sarıkovanlık, V. (2022). Forecasting Bist100 and Nasdaq Indices with Single and Hybrid Machine Learning Algorithms. *Economic Computation and Economic Cybernetics Studies and Research*, *56*(3), 235–250. https://doi.org/10.24818/18423264/56.3.22.15.

Özgür, C. (2022). Blockchain Applications in Derivatives Markets (pp. 37–55). In S. Balı, M. Akkaya, & G. Topçu (Eds.) *Blockchain in Finance, Marketing and Others*. Nobel Bilimsel.

Pagliaro, C., Mehta, D., Shiao, H. T., Wang, S., & Xiong, L. (2021). Investor Behavior Modeling by Analyzing Financial Advisor Notes: A Machine Learning Perspective. *arXiv*, *arXiv:2107.05592v1*. https://doi.org/10.48550/arXiv.2107.05592.

Paiva, F. D., Cardoso, R. T. N., Hanaoka, G. P., & Duarte, W. M. (2019). Decision-Making for Financial Trading: A Fusion Approach of Machine Learning and Portfolio Selection. *Expert Systems with Applications*, *115*, 635–655. https://doi.org/10.1016/j.eswa.2018.08.003.

Pakhchanyan, S., Fieberg, C., Metko, D., & Kaspereit, T. (2022). Machine Learning for Categorization of Operational Risk Events Using Textual Description. *Journal of Operational Risk*, *17*(4), 37–65. https://doi.org/10.21314/JOP.2022.026.

Papenbrock, J., Schwendner, P., Jaeger, M., & Krügel, S. (2021). Matrix Evolutions: Synthetic Correlations and Explainable Machine Learning for Constructing Robust Investment Portfolios. *The Journal of Financial Data Science*, *3*(2), 51–69.

Pena, A., Patino, A., Chiclana, F., Caraffini, F., Gongora, M., Gonzalez-Ruiz, J. D., & Duque-Grisales, E. (2021). Fuzzy Convolutional Deep-Learning Model to Estimate the Operational Risk Capital Using Multi-Source Risk Events. *Applied Soft Computing*, *107*, 107381. https://doi.org/10.1016/j.asoc.2021.107381.

Poole, D., Mackworth, A., & Goebel, R. (1998). *Computational Intelligence: A Logical Approach*. Oxford University Press.

Qianyun, Y., & Xiaoyan, W. (2021). Simulation of Stock Market Investor Behavior Based on Bayesian Learning and Complex Network. *Journal of Intelligent & Fuzzy Systems*, *40*(2), 2481–2491.

Quinlan, J. R. (1986). Induction of Decision Trees. *Machine Learning*, *1*, 81–106.

Owen, S. R. (2023). An Analysis of Conditional Mean-Variance Portfolio Performance Using Hierarchical Clustering. *The Journal of Finance and Data Science*, *9*, 100112. https://doi.org/10.1016/j.jfds.2023.100112.

Ramos-Pérez, E., Alonso-González, P. J., & Núñez-Velázquez, J. J. (2019). Forecasting Volatility with a Stacked Model Based on a Hybridized Artificial Neural Network. *Expert Systems with Applications*, *129*, 1–9. https://doi.org/10.1016/j.eswa.2019.03.046.

Ravi, V., Chauhan, N. J., & Kıran, N. J. (2009). Software Reliability Prediction Using Intelligent Techniques: Application to Operational Risk Prediction in Firms. *International Journal of Computational Intelligence and Applications*, *8*(2), 181–194. https://doi.org/10.1142/S1469026809002588.

Rizinski, M., Peshov, H., Mishev, K., Chitkushev, L. T., Vodenska, I., & Trajanov, D. (2022). Ethically Responsible Machine Learning in Fintech. *IEEE Access*, *10*, 97531–97554. https://doi.org/10.1109/ACCESS.2022.3202889.

Rizinski, M., Peshov, H., Mishev, K., Jovanovik, M., & Trajanov, D. (2024). Sentiment Analysis in Finance: From Transformers Back to eXplainable Lexicons (XLex). *IEEE Access*, *12*, 7170–7198. https://doi.org/10.1109/ACCESS.2024.3349970.

Rosenblatt, F. (1957). The Perceptron: A Perceiving and Recognizing Automaton. *Project Para, Cornell Aeronautical Laboratory*, Report no 85–60–1.

Rosenblatt, F. (1962). *Principles of Neurodynamics: Perceptrons and the Theory of Brain Mechanisms*. Spartan.

Roy, J. K., & Vasa, L. (2024). Machine Learning and Artificial Intelligence Method for FinTech Credit Scoring and Risk Management: A Systematic Literature Review. *International Journal of Business Analytics*, *11*(1), 1–23. https://doi.org/10.4018/IJBAN.347504.

Russell, S. J., & Norvig, P. (2020). *Artificial Intelligence: A Modern Approach* (4th ed.). Pearson Education, Inc.

Sadgali, I., Sael, N., & Benabbou, F. (2018). Detection of Credit Card Fraud: State of Art. *International Journal of Computer Science and Network Security*, *18*(11), 76–83.

Sahu, S. K., Mokhade, A., & Bokde, N. D. (2023). An Overview of Machine Learning, Deep Learning, and Reinforcement Learning-Based Techniques in Quantitative Finance: Recent Progress and Challenges. *Applied Sciences*, *13*(3), 1956. https://doi.org/10.3390/app13031956.

Sakarya, Ş., & Aksu, M. (2021). Fintech Ecosystem in Turkey: An Evaluation in Terms of Financial Markets and Financial Stability (Vol. 1, pp. 11–31). In S. B. Kahyaoğlu (Ed.)

The Impact of Artificial Intelligence on Governance, Economics and Finance. Springer Nature. https://doi.org/10.1007/978-981-33-6811-8_2.

Samuel A. L. (1959). Some Studies in Machine Learning Using the Game of Checkers. *IBM Journal of Research and Development*, *3*(3), 210–29.

Sanga, B., & Aziakpono, M. (2023). FinTech and SMEs Financing: A Systematic Literature Review and Bibliometric Analysis. *Digital Business*, *3*, 100067. https://doi.org/10.1016/j.digbus.2023.100067.

Sangwan, V. H., Prakash, P., & Singh, S. (2020). Financial Technology: A Review of Extant Literature. *Studies in Economics and Finance*, *37*(1), 71–88. https://doi.org/10.1108/SEF-07-2019-0270.

Sharma, S. K., Ilavarasan, P. V., & Karanasios, S. (2024). Small Businesses and FinTech: A Systematic Review and Future Directions. *Electronic Commerce Research*, *24*, 535–575. https://doi.org/10.1007/s10660-023-09705-5.

Shou, M., Bao, X., & Yu, J. (2021). An Optimal Weighted Machine Learning Model for Detecting Financial Fraud. *Applied Economics Letters*, *30*(4), 410–415. https://doi.org/10.1080/13504851.2021.1989367.

Silva, T. C., Tabak, B. M., & Ferreira, I. M. (2019). Modeling Investor Behavior Using Machine Learning: Mean-Reversion and Momentum Trading Strategies. *Complexity*, *1*, 4325125. https://doi.org/10.1155/2019/4325125.

Snow, D. (2020a). Machine Learning in Asset Management—Part 1: Portfolio Construction—Trading Strategies. *The Journal of Financial Data Science*, *2*(1), 10–23. https://doi.org/10.3905/jfds.2019.1.021.

Snow, D. (2020b). Machine Learning in Asset Management—Part 2: Portfolio Construction—Weight Optimization. *The Journal of Financial Data Science*, *2*(2), 17–24.

Soori, M., Arezoo, B., & Dastres, R. (2023). Artificial Intelligence, Machine Learning and Deep Learning in Advanced Robotics, a Review. *Cognitive Robotics*, *3*, 54–70. https://doi.org/10.1016/j.cogr.2023.04.001.

Stojanović, B., Božić, J., Hofer-Schmitz, K., Nahrgang, K., Weber, A., Badii, A., Sundaram, M., Jordan, E., & Runevic, J. (2021). Follow the Trail: Machine Learning for Fraud Detection in Fintech Applications. *Sensors*, *21*(5), 1594. https://doi.org/10.3390/s21051594.

Su, Y., Qu, Y., & Kang, Y. (2021). Online Public Opinion and Asset Prices: A Literature Review. *Data Science in Finance and Economics*, *1*(1), 60–76. https://doi.org/10.3934/DSFE.2021004.

Tipping, M. E. (2001). Sparse Bayesian Learning and the Relevance Vector Machine. *Journal of Machine Learning Research*, *1*, 211–244.

Todd, A., Bowden, J., & Moshfeghi, Y. (2024). Text-Based Sentiment Analysis in Finance: Synthesizing the Existing Literature and Exploring Future Directions. *Intelligent Systems in Accounting, Finance and Management*, *31*(1), e1549. https://doi.org/10.1002/isaf.1549.

Treleaven, P., Galas, M., & Lalchand, V. (2013). Algorithmic Trading Review. *Communications of ACM*, 56, 76–85.

Tsai, C. F. (2009). Feature Selection in Bankruptcy Prediction. *Knowledge-Based Systems*, *22*(2), 120–127. https://doi.org/10.1016/j.knosys.2008.08.002.

Van de Kauter, M., Breesch, D., & Hoste, V. (2015). Fine-Grained Analysis of Explicit and Implicit Sentiment in Financial News Articles. *Expert Systems with Applications*, *42*(11), 4999-5010. https://doi.org/10.1016/j.eswa.2015.02.007.

van Engelen, J. E., & Hoos, H. H. (2020). A Survey on Semi-Supervised Learning. *Machine Learning*, *109*, 373–440. https://doi.org/10.1007/s10994-019-05855-6.

Virgilio, G. P. M. (2019). High-Frequency Trading: A Literature Review. *Financial Markets and Portfolio Management*, *33*, 183–208. https://doi.org/10.1007/s11408-019-00331-6.

Vo, N. N., He, X., Liu, S., & Xu, G. (2019). Deep Learning for Decision Making and the Optimization of Socially Responsible Investments and Portfolio. *Decision Support Systems*, *124*, 113097. https://doi.org/10.1016/j.dss.2019.113097.

Wang, N. (2017). Bankruptcy Prediction Using Machine Learning. *Journal of Mathematical Finance*, 7, 908–918. https://doi.org/10.4236/jmf.2017.74049.

Wang, J., Jiang, C., Zhang, H., Ren, Y., Chen, K.-C., & Hanzo, L. (2020). Thirty Years of Machine Learning: The Road to Pareto-Optimal Wireless Networks. *IEEE Communications Surveys & Tutorials*, *2*(3), 1472–1514. https://doi.org/ 10.1109/COMST.2020.2965856.

Wang, W., Li, W., Zhang, N., & Liu, K. (2020). Portfolio Formation with Preselection Using Deep Learning from Long-Term Financial Data. *Expert Systems with Applications*, *143*, 113042. https://doi.org/10.1016/j.eswa.2019.113042.

Wang, Y., & Yan, G. (2021). Survey on the Application of Deep Learning in Algorithmic Trading. *Data Science in Finance and Economics, 1*(4), 345–361. https://doi.org/ 10.3934/DSFE.2021019.

Weigand, A. (2019). Machine Learning in Empirical Asset Pricing. *Financial Markets and Portfolio Management*, *33*, 93–104. https://doi.org/10.1007/s11408-019-00326-3.

Yang, X., Song, Z., King, I., & Xu, Z. (2023). A Survey on Deep Semi-Supervised Learning. *IEEE Transactions on Knowledge and Data Engineering*, *35*(9), 8934–8954. https://doi.org/10.1109/TKDE.2022.3220219.

Yao, J., Li, Y., & Tan, C. L. (2000). Option Price Forecasting Using Neural Networks. *Omega, 28*, 455–466. https://doi.org/10.1016/S0305-0483(99)00066-3.

Yeh, I-C., & Lien, C.-h. (2009). The Comparisons of Data Mining Techniques for the Predictive Accuracy of Probability of Default of Credit Card Clients. *Expert Systems with Applications*, *36*, 2473–80.

Yu, L., Wang, S., & Lai, K. K. (2008). Credit Risk Assessment with a Multistage Neural Network Ensemble Learning Approach. *Expert Systems with Applications*, *34*(2), 1434–1444. https://doi.org/10.1016/j.eswa.2007.01.009.

Zeng, X., Li, Y., Leung, S. C., Lin, Z., & Liu, X. (2016). Investment Behavior Prediction in Heterogeneous Information Network. *Neurocomputing*, *217*, 125–132. https://doi.org/10.1016/j.neucom.2015.12.139.

Zhang, J., & Chen, X. (2021). Socially Responsible Investment Portfolio Construction with a Double-Screening Mechanism considering Machine Learning Prediction. *Discrete Dynamics in Nature and Society*, *2021*(1), 7390887. https://doi.org/10.1155/2021/ 7390887.

Zhang, Z., Zohren, S., & Roberts, S. (2020). Deep Learning for Portfolio Optimization. *The Journal of Financial Data Science*, *2*(4), 8–20. https://doi.org/10.3905/jfds.2020.1.042.

Zhou, Z.-H. (2012). *Ensemble Methods: Foundations and Algorithms*. CRC Press.

Zhou, F., Qi, X., Xiao, C., & Wang, J. (2021). MetaRisk: Semi-Supervised Few-Shot Operational Risk Classification in Banking Industry. *Information Sciences*, *552*, 1–16. https://doi.org/10.1016/j.ins.2020.11.027

About the Editors

Dr. Cemile Özgür

Cemile ÖZGÜR is currently a part-time lecturer at Boğaziçi University, Department of Management Information Systems. She obtained her undergraduate degree at Hacettepe University, Department of Business Administration. In 2014, she received her Master of Science in economics and finance at Rhine-Waal University of Applied Sciences in Germany, where she also undertook various academic activities, such as being a tutor, scientific assistant, and lecturer for the period of 2012–2016. In 2017, she continued her academic research at Istanbul University, Department of Finance and obtained a PhD degree in Finance in 2022.
E-mail: cemile.ozgur@pt.bogazici.edu.tr / ozgurcemile@yahoo.com
ORCID: 0000-0001-8366-6745

Dr. Vedat Sarikovanlik

Professor at Istanbul University, Faculty of Business Administration, Department of Finance since 2013. Vedat SARIKOVANLIK completed his secondary and high school education at Italian High School and his undergraduate degree at Boğaziçi University, Department of Business Administration. Vedat SARIKOVANLIK received his MSc and PhD degrees from Istanbul University, Department of Finance, and an MBA degree from Miller College, Ball State (IN), USA, in 2001. Vedat SARIKOVANLIK, who has worked as a trainer, consultant, and project manager in many companies and organizations, is the father of two daughters and is fluent in Italian and English. He is currently the Head of the Department of Finance at Istanbul University, Faculty of Business Administration.
E-mail: vedsari@istanbul.edu.tr
ORCID: 0000-0002-7152-6275

About the Contributors

Dr. Mahammad Charkasov

Dr. Mahammad CHARKASOV, born in Azerbaijan, is an academic specializing in finance and investment research. He began his educational journey in Türkiye, completing his undergraduate studies in the Insurance Department at Marmara University and subsequently earning a master's degree in finance from Istanbul University. He continued his academic path with a scholarship awarded under the "State Program on Increasing the International Competitiveness of the Higher Education System in the Republic of Azerbaijan" through which he pursued his doctoral studies. Focusing on portfolio management, financial markets, and exchange rate dynamics, CHARKASOV devoted his doctoral research to examining the applicability of algorithmic approaches in portfolio optimization. His work offers an innovative perspective by blending traditional finance theories with modern technological methodologies. Upon completing his doctorate, he joined Khazar University in Baku, Azerbaijan, where he now serves as a faculty member. In this role, he teaches both undergraduate and graduate courses while conducting academic research on behalf of the university.
E-mail: mcharkasov@khazar.org
ORCID: 0009-0004-1017-0510

Dr. Merve PERÇİN

Dr. Merve PERÇİN is a research assistant at Istanbul University, Faculty of Business Administration, Department of Finance. After receiving her bachelor's degree in economics from Boğaziçi University, she completed her master's and doctoral studies at Istanbul University, Department of Finance. Her research interests include international finance, international economics,

portfolio theory, and artificial intelligence in banking and finance. Her work has been published in national and international academic sources, and she is involved in various academic projects.
E-mail: merve.percin@istanbul.edu.tr
ORCID: 0000-0002-2727-9190

Index

U

V